Pasture Lawn
Y.2.

Dairy Meadow
Y.9.

Y.1.

Great
Hall Field.
Y.8.

Home
Pightel.
Y.10.

The Walk
Y.6.

Little
Hall-Field.
Y.7.

Middle Pightel
Y.11.

Three Acre Field.
Y.20.

Y.13.

Bush Field.

Well Pightel

Columbine Hall

Columbine Hall

*The story of a house
and its transformation*

Hew Stevenson
Leslie Geddes-Brown

Dove Books

First published 2018 by Dove Books
42 Canonbury Square
London N1 2AW

Text copyright © Hew Stevenson and Leslie Geddes-Brown except where indicated. Illustrations copyright © the copyright holders; see Picture Credits page 96.

All rights reserved. No part of this book may be reproduced, stored in a retrieval system, or transmitted in any form or by any means, electronic, mechanical, photocopying or otherwise without the prior permission of the copyright holders.

ISBN 978-1-902563-03-9
Typeset in Adobe Caslon Pro
Designed by Maggie Town
Printed by Healeys of Ipswich, England.

Cover photo by Kate Elliott
Endpapers from William Collier's map of Columbine Hall, 1741.

CONTENTS

Introduction 6

CHAPTER ONE
The Evacuee 8

CHAPTER TWO
The House 14

CHAPTER THREE
The Garden 26

CHAPTER FOUR
The Medieval Manor 46

CHAPTER FIVE
A Grand Time 56

CHAPTER SIX
The Working Farm 66

CHAPTER SEVEN
The Gig House and the West Barn 74

CHAPTER EIGHT
How it Was 80

Who We Are 90
Index 94
Acknowledgements & Picture Credits 96

Introduction

"... an ancient manor house of beauty standing straight out of the moat"
Norman Scarfe, *The Shell Guide to Suffolk,* 1960

The setting of Columbine Hall could hardly be more romantic. It was built in the late 14th century and stands surrounded by a wide and deep moat. It was the manor house of Thorney Columbers, on the outskirts of Stowupland village, two miles north east of Stowmarket. Over the centuries it has variously been referred to as Collyvers, Collumbarres and Columbers Hall but by the 19th century the name had settled down as Columbyne or Columbine Hall.

The house occupies the north west corner of a roughly square moated site of just under an acre. Its north and west wings stand at right angles to one another, their outer walls rising directly from the moat with the upper storey, timber-framed and lime-plastered, jettied out over the water. The east wing, a Regency red brick addition, projects towards the south, to make the house U-shaped, now enclosing a gravelled courtyard. The surrounding moat, about an acre of water, is continuous save for a single causeway (a bridge in ancient times) to the south which forms the approach to the house. From the south west, the house is reflected in the water surrounding it.

To the north, and beyond the moat, the land slopes gently down through green meadows towards the valley of the Gipping, a river that meanders its way west to Stowmarket, thence south into the Orwell and out into the sea at Ipswich. The meadows to the north, east and west once formed a park around the house.

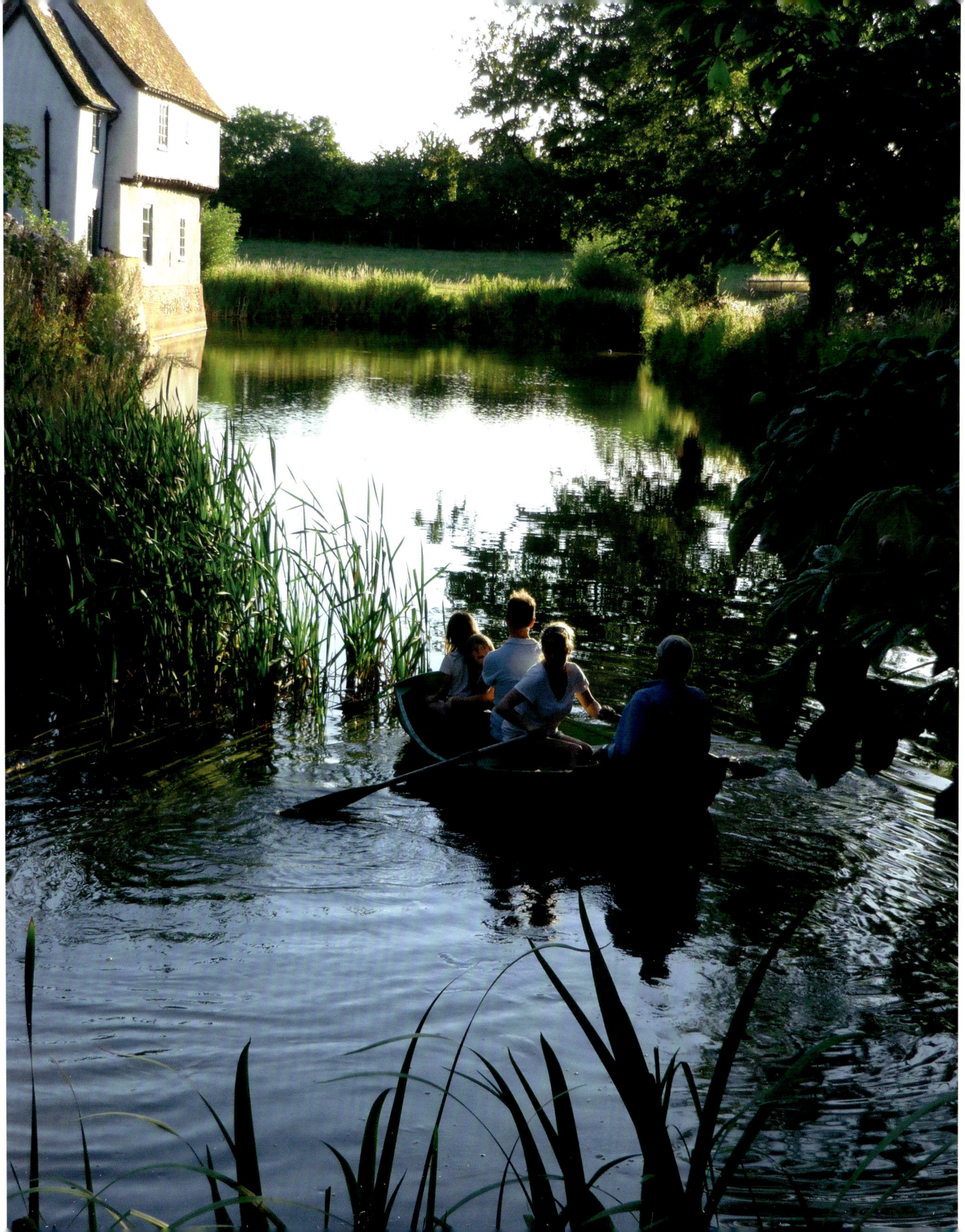

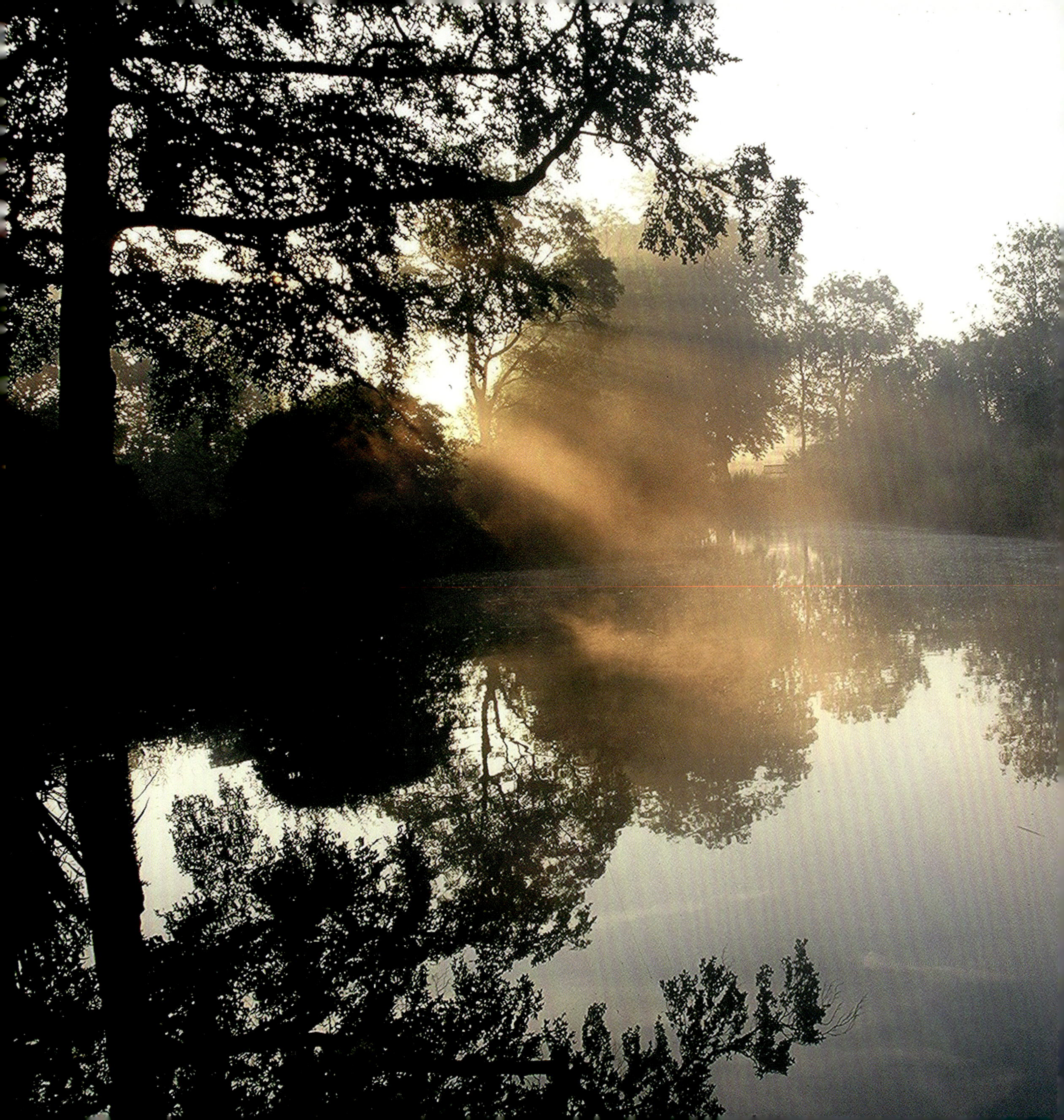

CHAPTER ONE

The Evacuee

Columbine Hall in wartime

With the advance of Hitler and the German army across Europe in 1939 the British government planned Operation Pied Piper, to evacuate thousands of children from vulnerable cities and billet them in homes in the country. As soon as war was declared between Britain and Germany in September that year, the plan was put into action.

Brian Hart, aged nine, and his friend Ian McPherson were billeted at Columbine Hall. Brian described his experience over 50 years later.

"The billeting officer, my mother, Ian McPherson and myself piled into his car, ending up on a very bumpy farm road. We drew up at a large farmhouse. We went in via the kitchen. The family were there to greet us – Mr. Potter, Mrs. Potter, Betty (11 years old) and John (7). I was to realise that we would be treated as part of the family.

It was not until the next morning that we realised that this was a 15th Century farmhouse. My mother called Ian and myself into her room and there across the moat were rabbits.

The house, Columbyne Hall, was in the shape of an 'E' with the middle bit missing. We went in and out by way of the kitchen (stable type) door. I never recall the 'front' door ever being opened. On the right-hand side of the kitchen as you went in were old built in "copper" boilers. Coats were usually left there and Mr. Potter's shotguns. Straight in front was a sink with a pump for water out of the moat. This was used very rarely. We used rain water collected in a barrel outside the kitchen for washing. Drinking water was brought down from a stand pipe on the main road on a four-wheeled railway trolley in churns. At nine, lifting full churns took some doing.

In the dairy we tried to make butter – hand churned. Mrs. Potter was an artist at this difficult task. Hanging up on the walls would be the latest shootings to mature. Pheasants, partridge, mallard, pigeon, hare, rabbit and even moorhen. If it moved and was edible, it was shot and eaten.

Turn right in the kitchen and there was the big black range. Through the doorway into the living room, two sides of which had windows overlooking the moat and the room was lit by oil lamps – no services laid on. The big fireplace also included another oven. Mrs. Potter was a great cook and nothing, but nothing, would be wasted and that included a heated oven.

Two doors led out from the living room, one directly on to a steep staircase winding up to the first floor. There were at least two bedrooms. One used by my mother for the few days at the

RIGHT Columbine Hall – September 1939 *From left:* John Potter, Brian Hart, Betty Potter, Ian McPherson and the Potters' cousin Pamela

PREVIOUS PAGES Mist rises from the moat early one morning.

beginning and on subsequent visits. The other faced the driveway and had a large bed in it. Ian and myself shared it. Later on it accommodated three of us – when Maurice King and George Shepherd replaced Ian McPherson. The disconcerting thing at first was the noises. The walls were made of lath and plaster and very old. Mice had made passageways and during the night we could hear 'scuttle, scuttle, squeak, squeak'. Bang on the wall and all hell would be let loose as the mice rustled in all directions. We soon learnt not to bang on the wall.

Outside, beyond the kitchen were various sheds, one of which contained the milk cooler. The milk for local use would be poured through this apparatus. Late in the afternoon the children from the houses and council bungalows on the main road would come with enamel containers. Milk has never tasted as good. Behind this range of sheds and huts was a cage which contained the ferrets. One game was to see if you could get your finger away before the ferret bit it. On the opposite side, behind that wing of the house was the toilet. It contained a good size in spiders and cut up copies of the East Anglian newspaper.

Over the unmade road that crossed the moat, were more rundown buildings. To the right were the stables which housed two horses, Dolly and Nigger. Dolly was a Suffolk mare, docile and easy-going. Nigger was a large black horse and a good deal more lively. They were looked after by Debla – I never knew his real name. He was the general farm hand and seemed to be related to Skipper who also worked on the farm as a sort of foreman. They lived in the council bungalows.

Debla was always dressed in an old sports jacket, corduroy trousers tied above the ankles and wearing an old hat. It was really enjoyable to go out in a tumbril with Dolly pulling even when we were muck spreading! Debla was a real countryman and his eyes and ears could see and hear what we couldn't. Nests would be pointed out which were invisible to a townee's eyes. Dolly would let us

THE EVACUEE   11

LEFT Columbine Hall – May 1940. Three evacuees with the Potter children. *From left:* Ian King, John Potter, Betty Potter, George Shephard and Brian Hart. (George Shephard was killed 20 years later in a pub brawl)

sit sideways on her back – the countryman's way of riding and it was only in later years that I was to appreciate the importance of touch with animals. Dolly's warm back and whiskers were a totally new experience for me.

I can vaguely remember a bad-tempered pig in a pen in the barn yard. If we went near he would rush over making a frightful row. It was not unusual to see rats about in the barns. Occasionally Mr. Potter would have a rat hunt with Bess, the black Newfoundland – not really a ratting dog but game to have a go. It was in this barn yard that Mr. P. cornered a large rat and I remember the red in the rat's eye and its bared yellow teeth as he was shot.

Across from the stables was the cow shed. Another task for young lads was to bring the cows in. How important we felt with our sticks and calls of "Hup back there!". Little did we know that the cows could find their own way in without much help from us. Once again, our energy was put to use instead of into mischief. It was opposite the cow shed and I believe another store barn that there were corn stacks – and this meant threshing.

For this we had time off school! The threshing gang with their traction engine and machinery turned up. As the ricks went down the boys had (to them) the important task of killing the mice and rats as they came out.

A dominant feature was the moat. This surrounded the house and immediate outbuildings, with a roadway in. It was stocked with roach and, so we believed, a large pike. Mallards would swim and quack under the windows of the house. In the severe 1939/40 winter the moat froze over. We had the biggest slide in the district and fish were actually frozen in the ice.

The farm itself was nearly 300 acres, mainly meadow and to us represented the ultimate in Cowboy and Indian country. At the bottom of the farm was a tributary of the River Gipping where watercress grew wild. The hedges provided plenty of wildlife and on Saturdays throughout the winter the local farmers organised a shoot. Every so often this came to Columbyne Hall and the boys would be given the task of carrying the sticks on which the game would be hung. Rabbits were the most frequent losers. We would get out of the way quickly when pheasants were flushed as all the farmers seemed to be good shots! Bess the dog seemed to enjoy the afternoon as much as anybody.

With hindsight, I now realise that the Potters were not well off and the money coming in from the evacuees helped the family purse. The Ministry of Ag & Fish seem to have visited the farm early in the war and the upshot was that the Potters left Columbyne Hall in 1941. His farm could not have been very productive even for the standards of the day. There was a farm sale and the top field had unwanted wagons in it until I left in May 1940. Those self-same wagons would now be worth considerable sums of money. The Potters moved to Debenham where Mr. Potter died quite suddenly in 1943 or 4.

I remember them as what must have been a typical farming couple of the time. Mrs. Potter was rarely without her wrap-around apron and always on the go. The washing must have been increased with the arrival of grubby, small boys. She, as so many other women at that time, was never still. Neither had any airs and graces and certainly did not go in for genteel living, yet a Christmas party when other farming friends came did justice to Charles Dickens. Held in the big room, it was an evening to remember of games and simple enjoyment. We went to a 'return match' somewhere. These must have been the only times that Mrs. Potter would dress up. Mr. Potter would put a collar and tie on to go to market. Normally his appearance was not much different to Skipper or Debla. Their daughter, Betty, was looked upon as slightly unusual. She had passed the scholarship to go to Stowmarket Grammar School – a rare event among the village children – proof that they weren't all slow in the uptake. Many of them could have done well but their whole reasoning was against "larnin". Who would have thought that this way of life would have disappeared in so short a time."

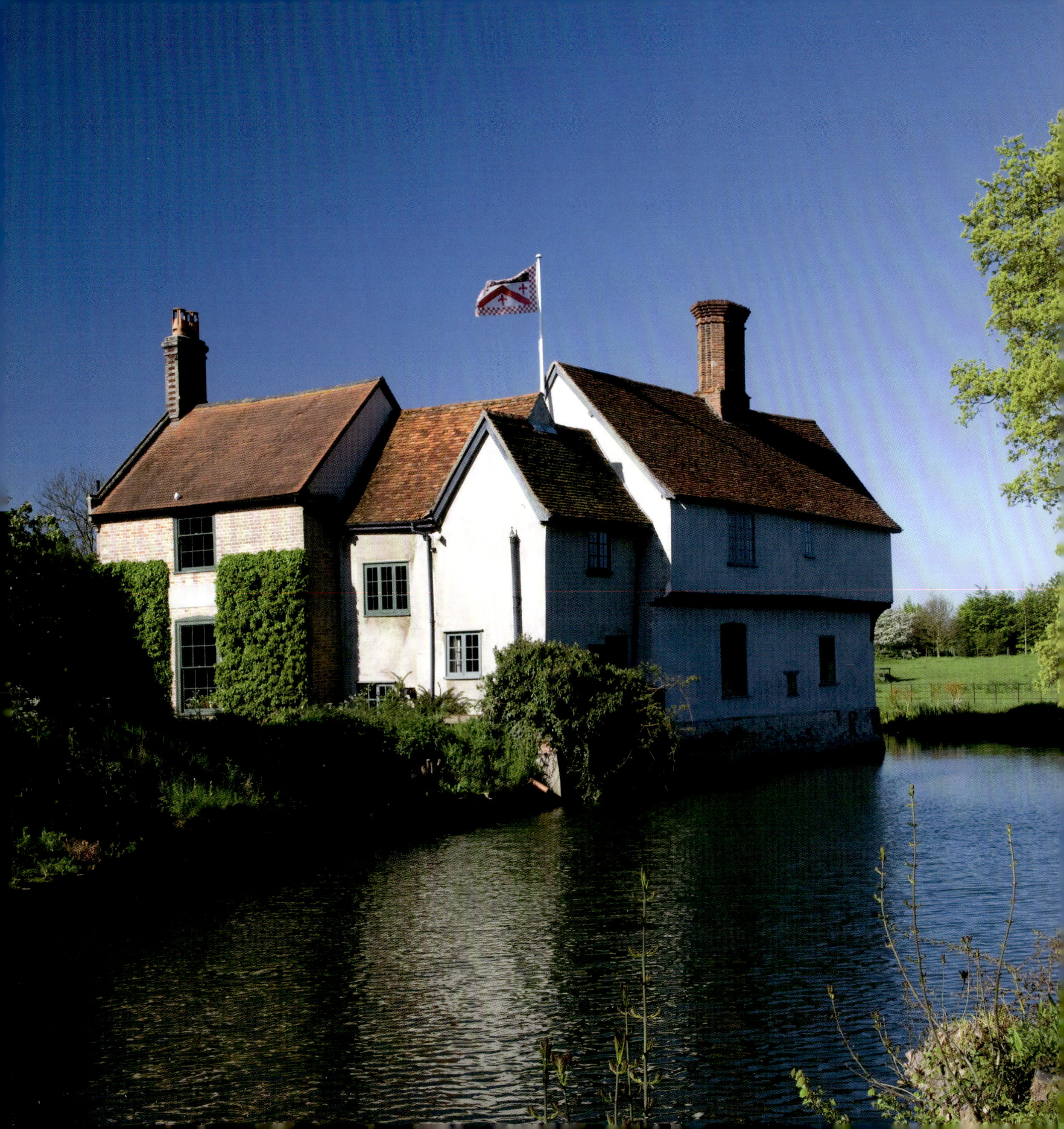

CHAPTER TWO

The House

Adapted from an article by Leslie Geddes-Brown published in *World of Interiors* November 2001, and reproduced with the editor's permission.

An "enchanting moated house"

James Bettley and Nikolaus Pevsner, *The Buildings of England, Suffolk West*, 2015

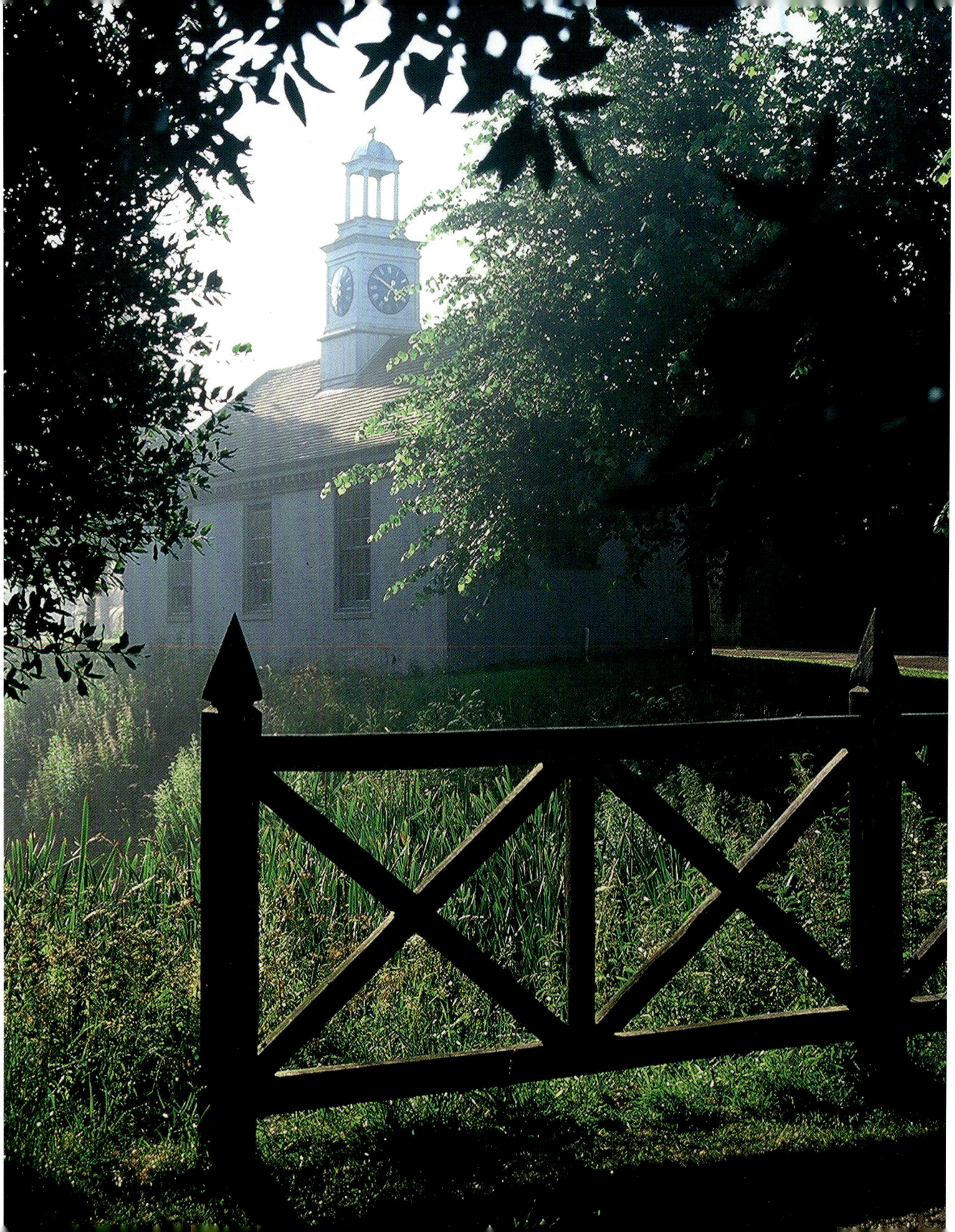

RIGHT The front hall being part of the Regency addition.
OPPOSITE The Clocktower on a misty morning seen from the Platform bridge.
PREVIOUS PAGES The house from its north side, flying the Stevenson flag.

Like the Chinese, I was brought up to revere age. For me, 19th century so-so; 18th century good; 17th century better. So when my husband, Hew, and I found a 14th-century house with a proper 30ft-wide moat for sale in Suffolk, we were elated. What's more, the architecture of its gatehouse wing could have been described as Rare, even Important.

But, as we drove away after seeing it for the first time one raw November afternoon in 1992, we shook our heads. The house had been empty for seven years and little changed for 40, but that was fine (no need to pay for, then rip out, the £40,000 fitted kitchen). It was the three acres of concrete and farm buildings, most of them made of jarring red brick and asbestos, the six rusting grain silos sitting on a launch pad of impenetrable concrete, the two museum-quality petrol pumps and the corrugated iron Nissen huts that were the problem. But with every house we visit (and they are legion) we apply our home-made formula: what would you do with it if you were forced to own it?

LEFT A 1741 map, bought at auction, shows the house and its lands.
RIGHT The garden was designed to create a courtyard at its front.

By the time we reached London, we were so enthusiastic that we went through the agonising business of sudden-death sealed bids before a phone call told Hew the house was ours. Hew is a researchaholic and, within a year, we knew every single owner, from Philip de Columbers, the Norman overlord who was given the land for services rendered (best not to ask), and the 'mesne lords', the de Hotot family, who were there in 1242. Robert de Hotot built our timber-framed house in 1390, allowing us to fill in his name on our mortgage form instead of Wimpey or Barratt. He was a big legal cheese, making it all the more strange that his descendant, Anne Hotot, married the son of Sir James Tyrell, a near neighbour and murderer (or not, depending on your viewpoint) of the Princes in the Tower.

By the time Elizabeth was on the throne, the owner was Sir John Poley, a warty Bardolph of a mercenary. He flossied the house up by adding the huge brick chimneys and a very strange oak staircase. Later owners included a rich iron merchant and his heiress daughter, who predictably married the Earl of Ashburnham. She was worth millions at today's rates but the portrait we have of her, by William Hoare of Bath, shows a lot of swanky red gown and lace and hands capable of strangling a sheep.

It wasn't until 1914 that the Ashburnhams sold the house on – to the Potter family, whose son Harry (I promise you) was tossed out during

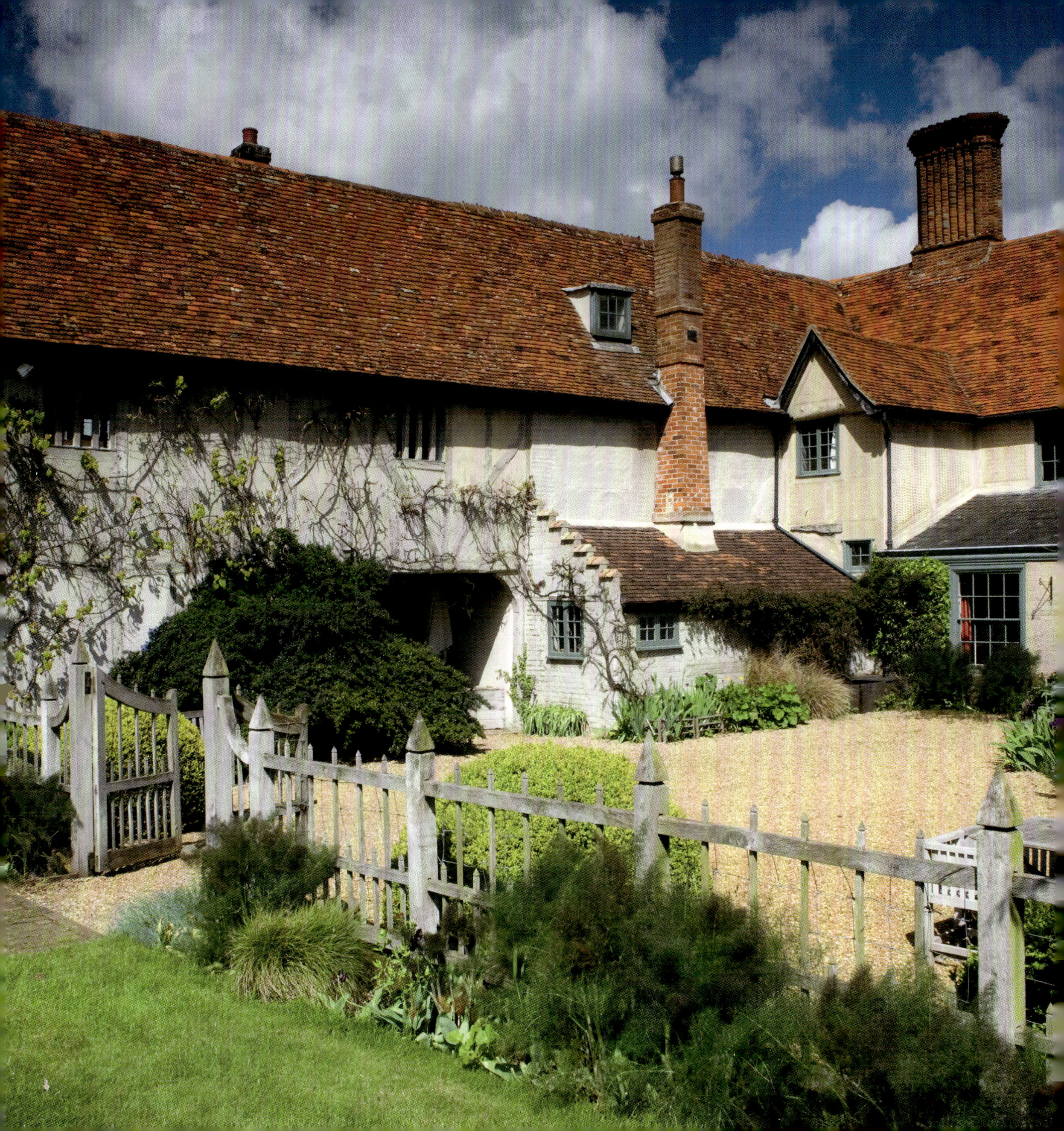

LEFT The Kitchen is in the medieval wing.
BELOW The Dining Room is hung with 19th century prints of the monarchs of England. The huge log-burning fire was reconstructed by Melvyn Smith.
OPPOSITE The Mud Room still had its disused Rayburn stove and butler's sink.

World War II by the Ministry of War for his unproductive farming habits. The farm, which had 240 acres later became a school for land girls – 40 of them; we have the remains of a massive septic tank to prove it. Every so often, one turns up to tell us how awful it was. When we dredged the moat we unearthed vast quantities of their tossed-away Marmite jars.

We bought the house from the Rednall family, farmers who moved in around 1950 and were reputed to order people off their land, shotgun in hand. Mrs Rednall, who died in the Eighties, was the last owner, notable for her insistence that the kitchen should be painted in gloss jasmine, the colour of pallid scrambled eggs, accessorised with gloss Quink-blue handles.

Having made our decision to buy, our first move was to ask Melvyn Smith, whom I'd met when the house he'd personally restored was featured in *World of Interiors* (Oct 1989), to come and crawl through every cobwebbed, rat-infested inch. What horrors lurked behind the grained doors and low Victorian ceilings? Were death-watch beetles killing the ancient oak beams and dry rot oozing up in the cellar? We knew he'd be rigorous with the truth because he'd be the man to deal with it. The reply was one word (he's not a man for hyperbole). It was 'wholesome.'

What we didn't reckon on was the marvellous discoveries behind the plasterboard: three Tudor brick fireplaces, a little the worse for wear; Medieval elm floorboards 18in wide, decorative ogee timber braces and the remains of mullioned windows hidden behind 17th century pargeting. We were also to learn all about the adaptability of timber frames which, though

20　COLUMBINE HALL

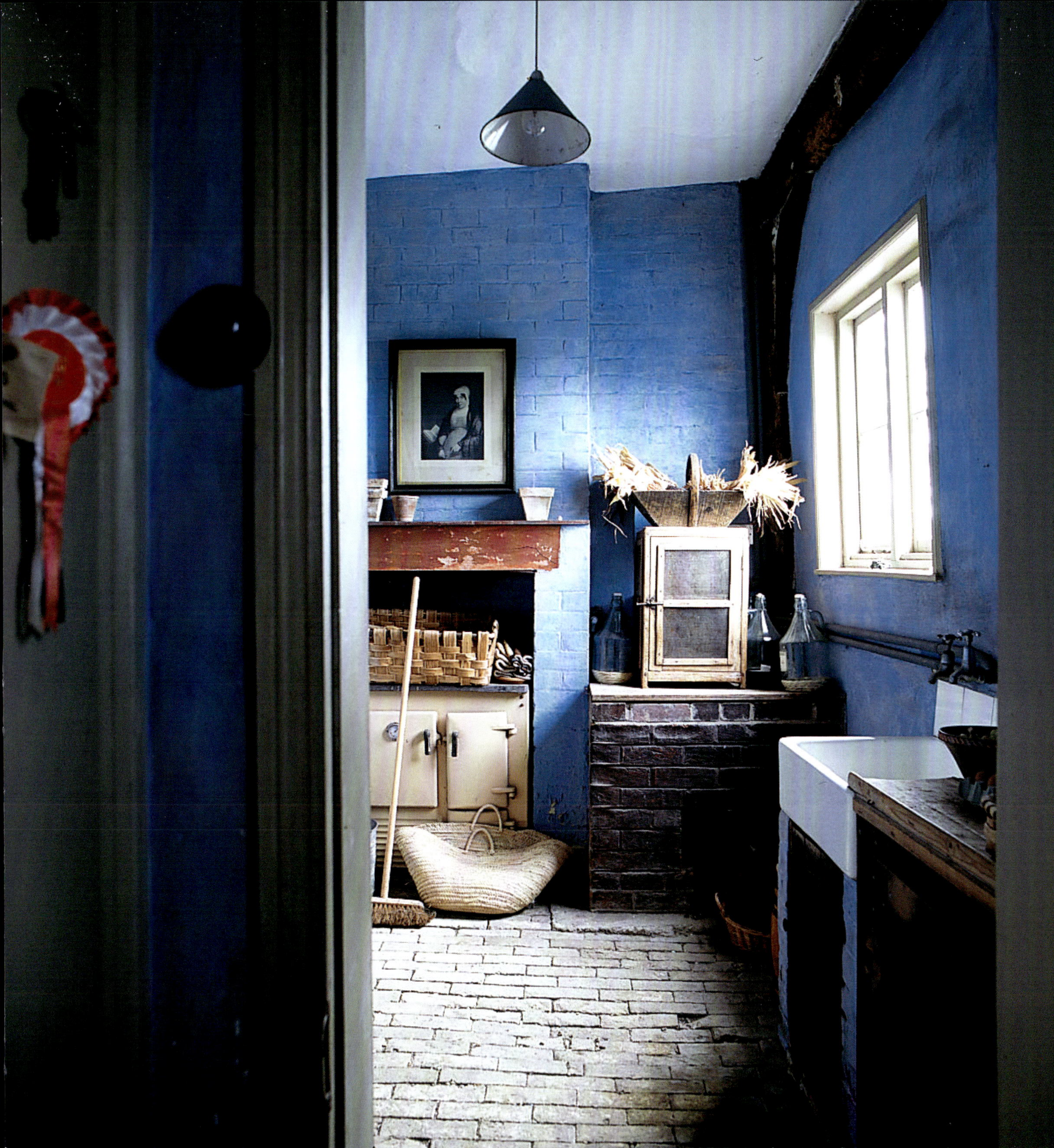

22　COLUMBINE HALL

they lean and creak like seagoing galleons, can always be hiked back into shape, and the way the complex beams reveal what was built when – and have names like 'splayed scarf joint with undersquinted abutment.' You can imagine Osric and Edgar, the Medieval carpenters, shouting such instructions to each other. Seemingly, our house was the minor, service end of something far grander that had already disappeared in 1741.

We didn't reckon – though as a past *Interiors* staffer I should have done – on how much could be invented or faked. Our drawing room is Regency outside and 1710 inside, the panelling having been created from scratch and MDF by Melvyn; panelling in one bathroom seems to have peg dowels to hold it together but these are, in fact, painted drawing pins. Our library shelves appear to have come from a Georgian townhouse, but these are another Melvyn production, assisted by antique enamel numbers for each book stack which were intended for a French clock.

ABOVE The Library, once a bedroom, has black and gold bookcases by Melvyn Smith. The full-size deer is Chinese.
LEFT Queen Anne-style panelling was added to the William IV extension, to turn it into a drawing room. A screen bearing the Stevenson arms guards the Delft-tiled fireplace. The "old master" lampshades are from Florence. The tables are all Chinese, as is the Tang horse on the mantelpiece.

LEFT Pictures of little girls hang on the walls in one of the bedrooms. The large one above the radiator is Hew's great great aunt Mary Stevenson. The hand-sewn quilts are from County Durham.
OPPOSITE The specially-built bed in the Sloping Floored Room. The patchwork quilt is Victorian.

Elsewhere, we've kept eccentricities, like the bit of metal tacked to a lavatory door to stop people peering through the key-hole to catch the naughty bits, the painted graining on an inbuilt Georgian cupboard, and a bedroom known, for obvious reasons, as the Sloping Floored Room. We even had a bed made to cope after we found we rolled out of bed as soon as we fell asleep.

Now we're tackling those acres of farm buildings that survived the purge that did away with the silos and petrol pumps. A new vegetable garden has risen from the walls of an asbestos-roofed horror, an ancient timbered barn is being baroqued up (by George Carter, who also designed our gardens and appeared in *Interiors* April 1990) to let out for parties, a Fifties farm office has been turned into a William and Mary cupola-ed eyecatcher, a gig house is ready for conversion into a holiday cottage, and a new pigeon loft to house the white doves is nearly complete. And no, we've not regretted turning our white elephant pink, not once for a moment.

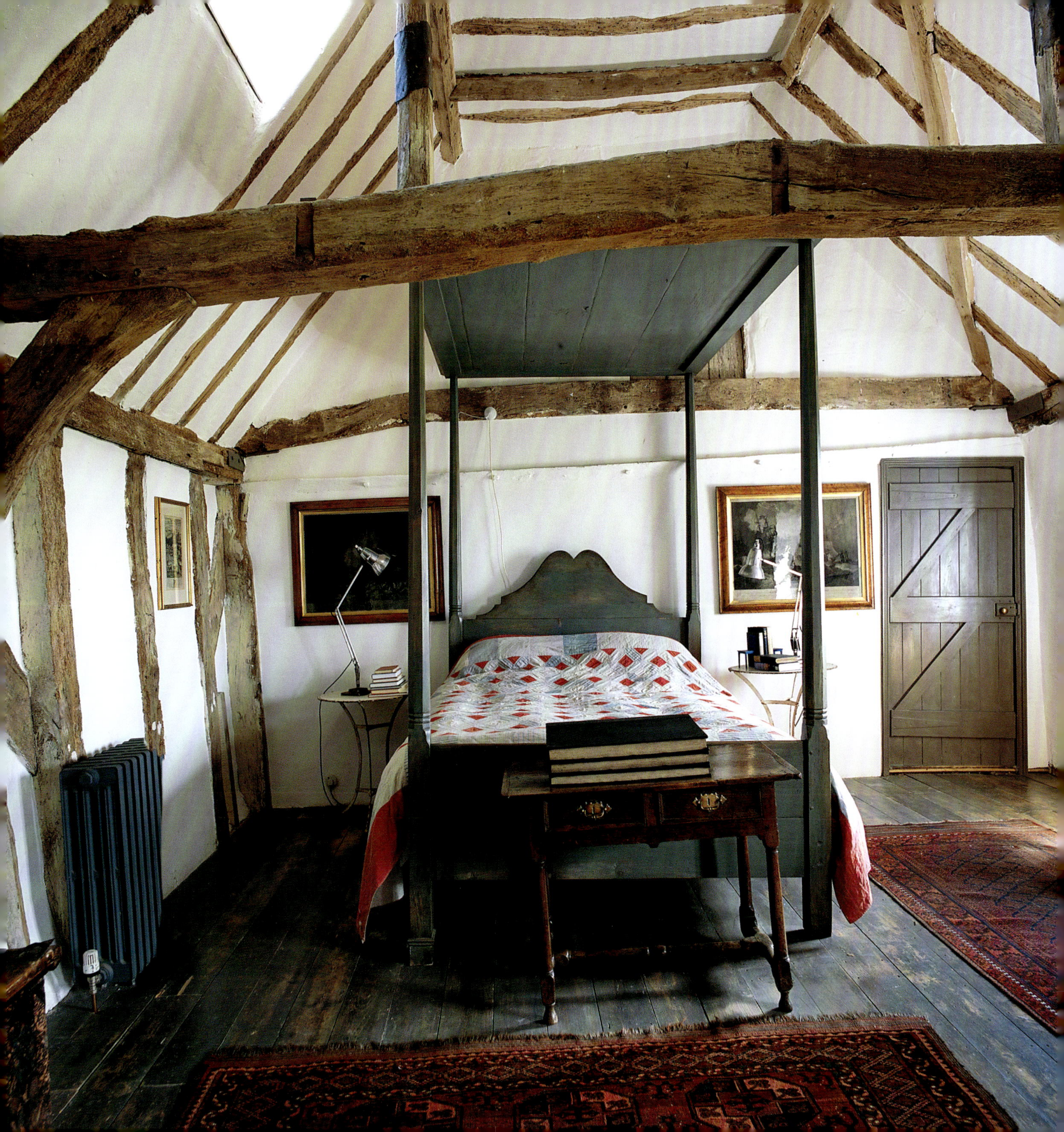

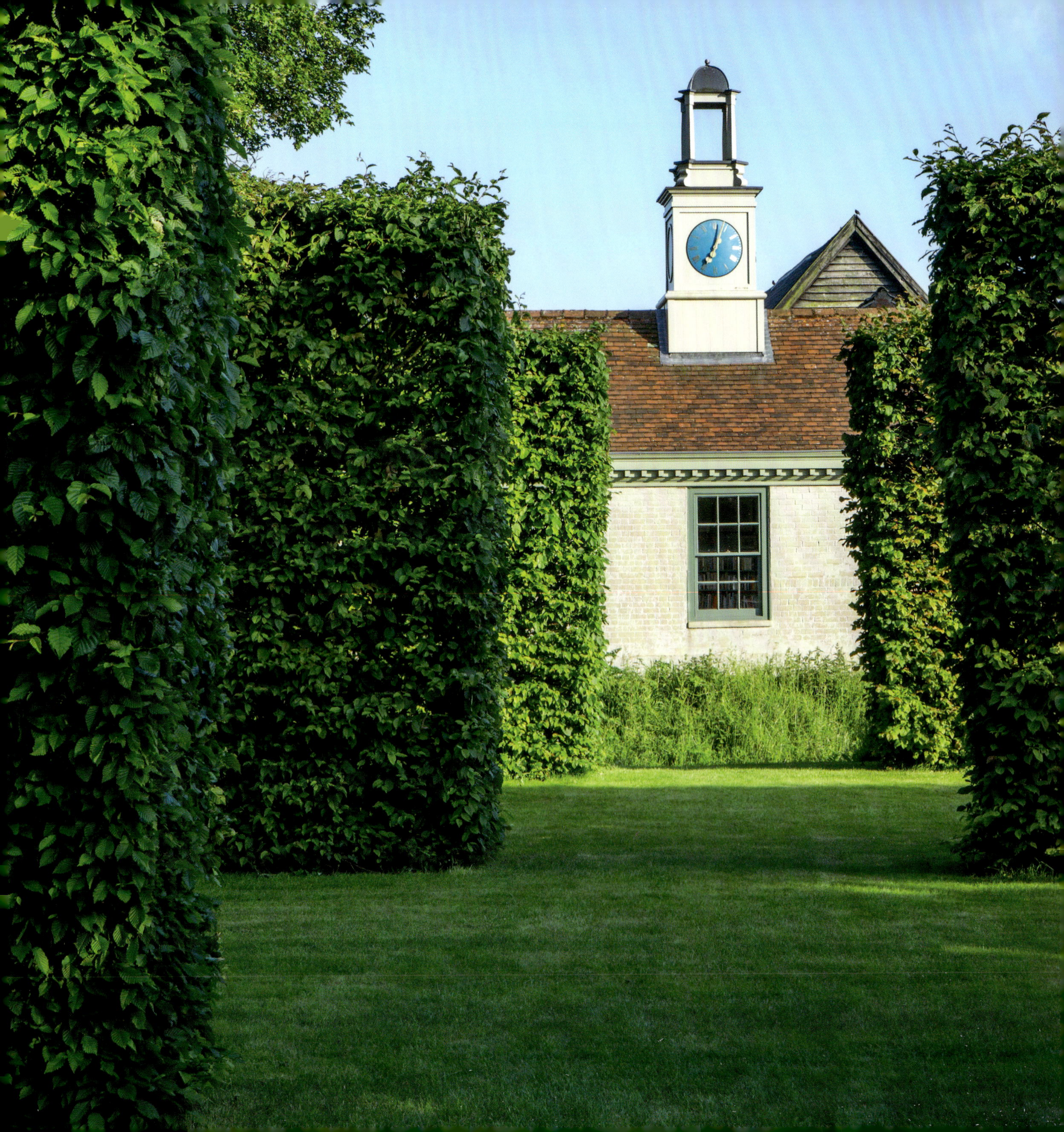

CHAPTER THREE

The Garden

"Islanded by its moat, in time as well as place, Columbine Hall's garden conveys a strong sense of history as well as poetry."

Roger Deakin, *Gardens Illustrated*, March 2002

PREVIOUS PAGES The Clock Tower, adapted from a dull 1960s farm office and dairy, seen through hornbeam hedges.
LEFT AND OPPOSITE George Carter's drawing of his suggested design, 1993.

Key to the Garden Plan (*opposite*)

A Columbine Hall
B Courtyard
C The Allée
D Bowling Green
E Herb Garden
F The Moat
G Clock Tower
H Walled Garden and Greenhouse
I Cart Sheds
J The Gig House
K The West Barn
L Half Moon Lawn
M Moat Walk
N Father Thames Spout
O Mediterranean Garden
P Bog Garden
Q New Orchard
R Lime Walk
S Wilderness
S Old Orchard

In 1993 Columbine Hall had no garden. The platform consisted of little more than a rough grassy gently sloping field crossed by the drive which ended in a turning circle in front of the house. We wanted a more formal layout with hedges and trees. We decided to act quickly so we asked our friend George Carter to come up with a plan.

George was concerned at the approach to the house; there was no sense of "arrival" he explained. He therefore proposed that the drive should pass through a series of openings along the way. He suggested that the causeway that crosses the moat should be flanked by wooden railings to give the impression you were crossing a bridge. A pair of ilex trees would then lead you through an opening in a formal yew hedge that would give on to a square gravelled area flanked on the west by the row of old outbuildings and planted with four formal lollipop hawthorn trees. A further opening in

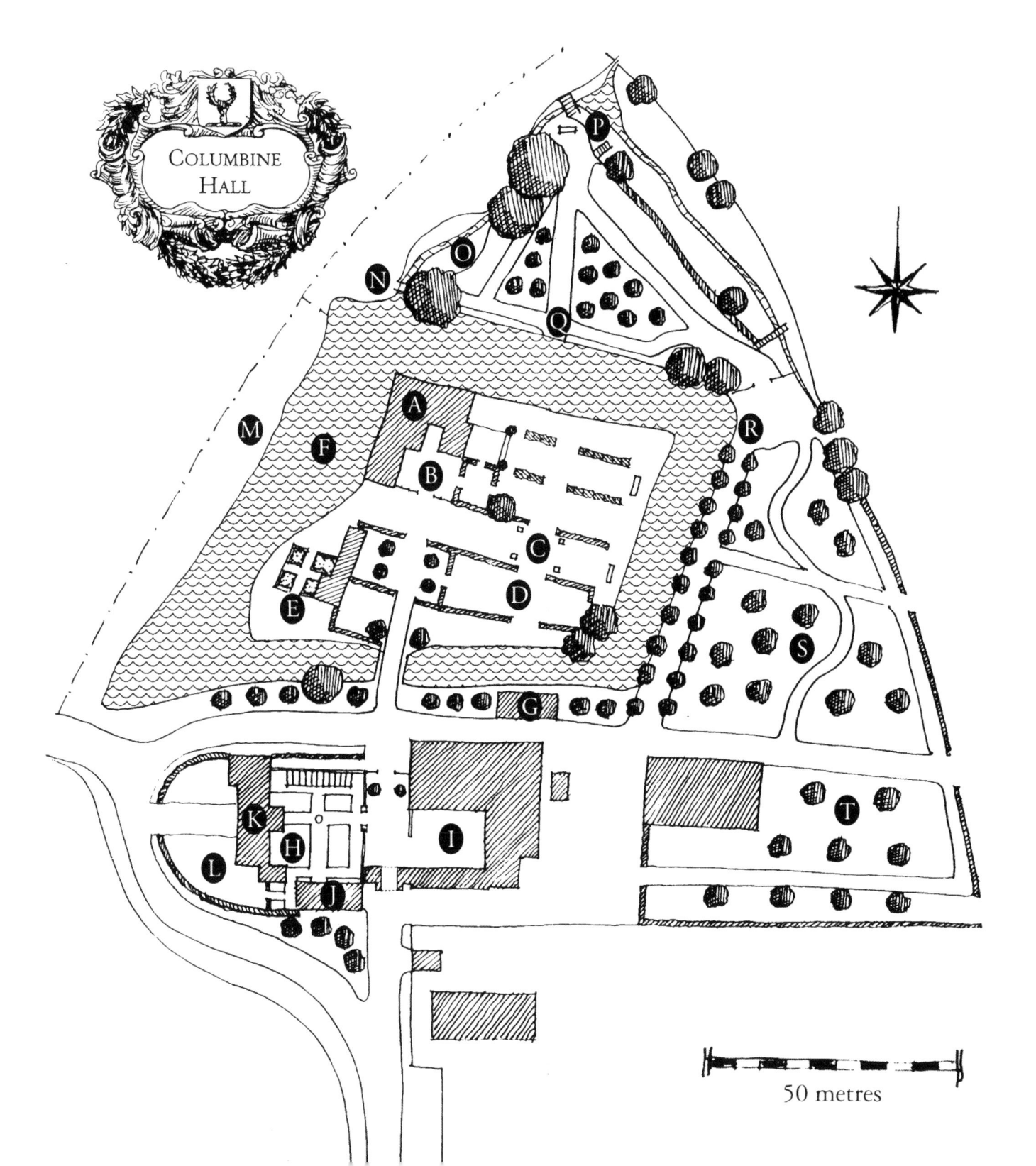

Columbine Hall

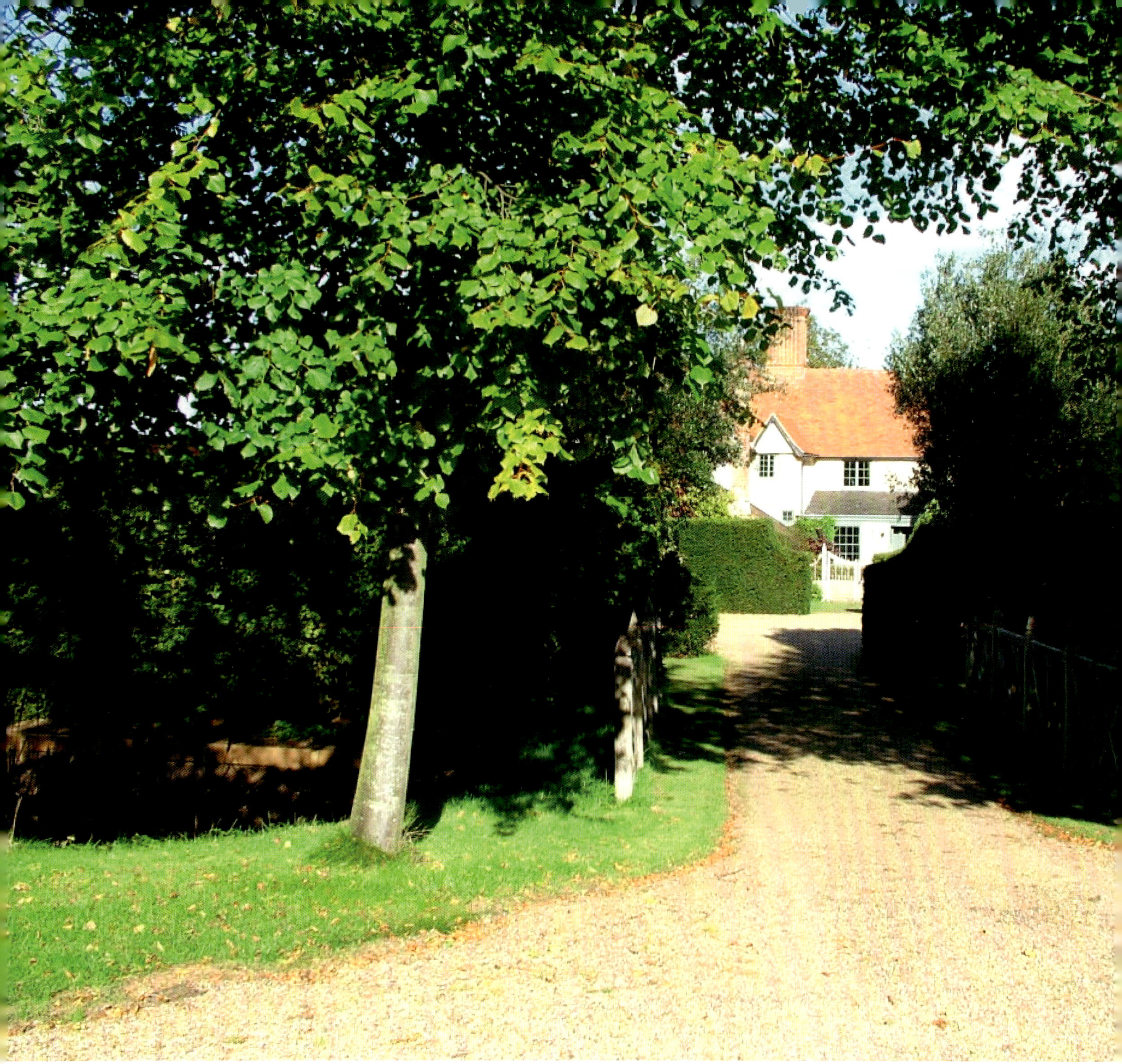

LEFT Formally-cut yew hedges lead the eye on from the causeway.

the yew hedge on the opposite side would take you along a short straight footpath to a gateway in oak fencing opening on to a final gravel courtyard at the house itself.

George, a trained sculptor, could see the land in 3D rather than just as a two-dimensional plan. The unsatisfactory slope of the platform, he said, should be corrected by making a series of terraces to create flat lawns and courtyards. However, he intended an uninterrupted grass sweep (the "allée") would follow the original slope of the land. This entailed some complex work by diggers to get the levels right.

Meanwhile, we had plans for other parts of the 29 acres. The western boundary was dominated by the view of the electricity supply line on the neighbouring farmer's land. It was bleak. With advice from Juliet Hawkins, a farm consultant, and helped by a grant from the Countryside Commission we planted a belt of woodland consisting of over 1000 trees, mostly native English species. The trees of course were tiny at first and needed watering and weeding to help them get established but have now developed into a proper wood, softening the landscape and providing a shelter belt against the prevailing west wind. Juliet also suggested planting pockets of woodland in some of the field corners. An essential part of our plan was to recreate the parkland that had surrounded the house in medieval times. The native English trees we planted in the meadows have now been there for 25 years so we now feel less pretentious when we refer to "The Park" – especially when it is grazed in the summer by our neighbour's Red Poll cattle.

The platform itself, apart from the approach to the house with its yew enclosure and gravelled areas, would consist mainly of mown grass subdivided by hornbeam hedges. A pleached lime avenue would line up with the drawing room window while eight narrow formal flower beds would be planted in blocks designed to imitate one of those gentleman's ties of the 1960s that had wide horizontal stripes. Herbaceous planting

THE GARDEN   31

ABOVE One of a set of four mossy urns by a hornbeam hedge.
LEFT The iron gate is French and frames a distant vista.
OPPOSITE The Lime Walk.

was restricted to these eight beds while the Allée and the Bowling Green would be left, understated, as plain lawned rooms. Strategically placed gaps in the hornbeam hedges would give vistas into the park and the countryside beyond.

The approach to the house passed through a farmyard between two huge asbestos-roofed sheds. But before you reached them George Carter proposed a high clapboarded archway flanked by matching outbuildings that linked with the 18th century ones. The gable above the arch would become a dovecot and before long the white doves that had inhabited the outbuildings for many years made it their home.

We removed the roofs of the two asbestos-roofed sheds and lowered their walls to make, on the east side, a gravelled courtyard. But the west side presented a bigger challenge. Here, the shed abutted and obscured two attractive 18th century timber framed farm buildings, the West Barn and what is now the Gig House holiday cottage. Once the asbestos roof was

THE GARDEN 33

"The other really exciting point about the garden is the journey that you are invited to make round the house . . . the circuit completes itself with the Moat Walk and the house seen from its really knockout side, reflected upside down even on an overcast day."
Catherine Howard, *Essential Suffolk*, March 2015

taken off and the walls reduced in height, the massive concrete floor had to be broken up and drainage pipes inserted (to take surplus rain water to the moat). We then imported a mass of topsoil, manure and dredgings from the moat to create what is now the Walled Garden. This is divided into four colour-themed squares planted with inspiration by our gardener, Kate Elliott.

The moat was badly silted up when we bought Columbine Hall in 1993. Reed mace had taken over nearly all the south east arm where the water was hardly visible. We had it dredged by a huge crane working its way round. We could hardly contain our excitement as we imagined the Viking helmets, and Saxon swords that we were sure would be discovered. Among the dredgings, however, were two rusty old medieval keys and 86 Marmite jars – the relics, we assumed, from the land girls' occupation during the war.

The moat is fed, at its south west corner, by an underground pipe leading off surrounding field ditches. Its outlet, in its north west corner, dribbles through a series of graduated ponds into a stream (little more than a ditch in summer) that runs north down the valley eventually to join the River Gipping.

Hew Stevenson

RIGHT The best-known view of Columbine Hall, its west front jettied over the wide moat. The bridge at the far end crosses the outlet.

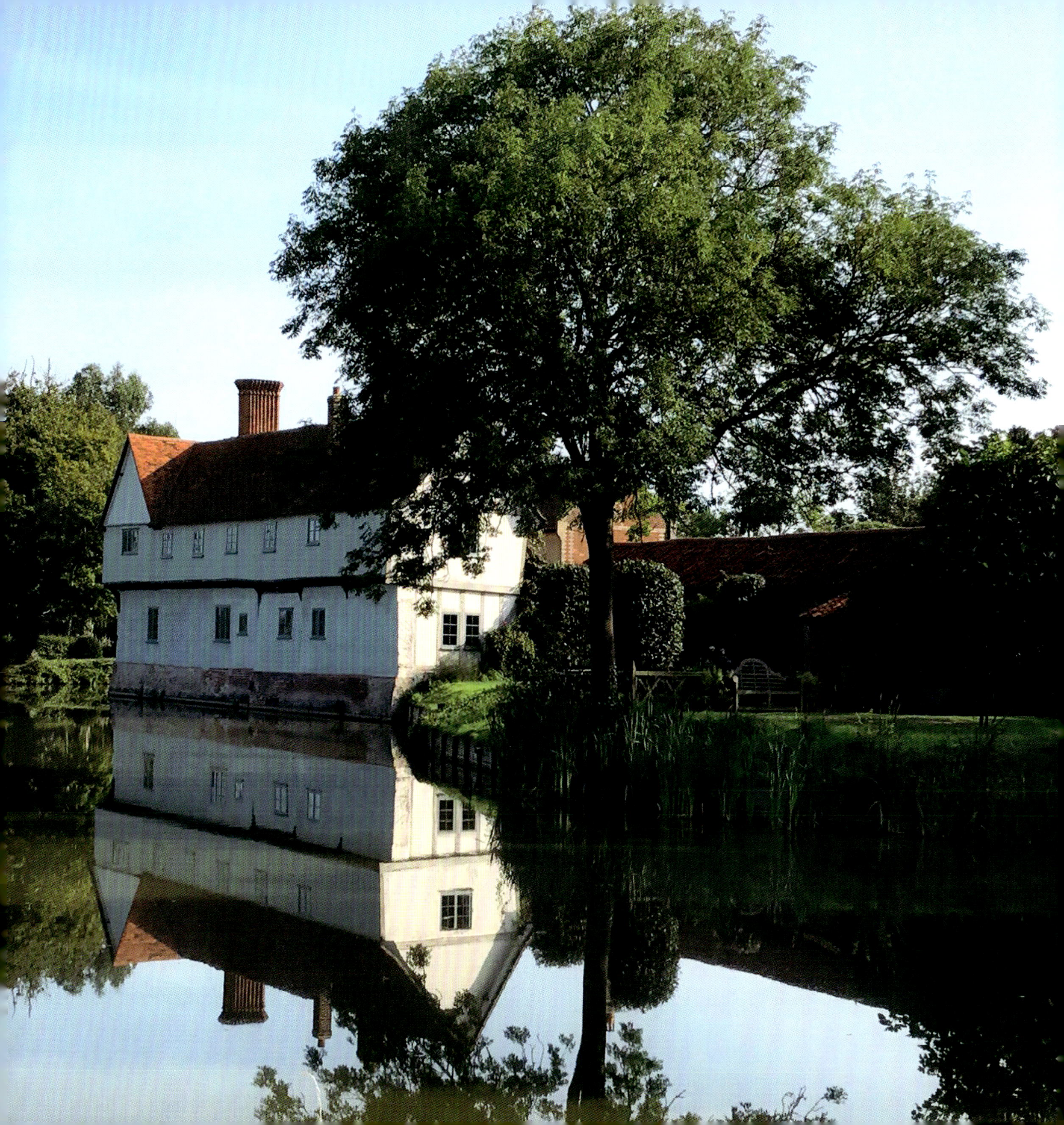

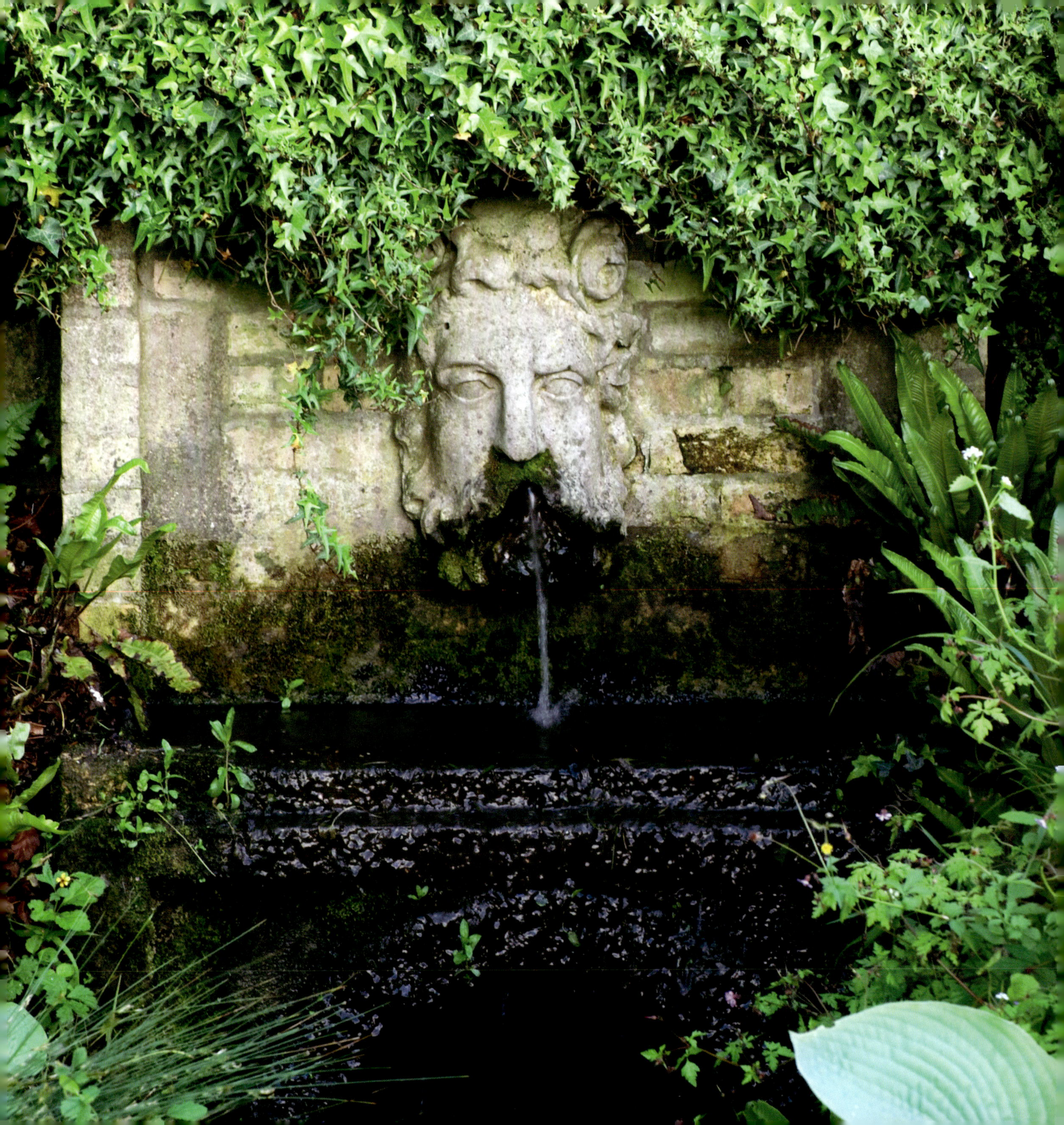

The Garden at Columbine Hall

Adapted from an article by Leslie Geddes-Brown published in *Country Life*, 27th April 2016, and reproduced with the editor's permission.

LEFT Water is a major feature of the garden. The 'spitting head' surrounded by ivy is of Father Thames.
ABOVE The lead water spout of a sheep's head is just beside the house. Its trickles can be heard indoors.

When you move house, do you look for one with a flourishing and beautiful garden or one festooned with elephant-high docks and nettles? My husband, Hew, and I never had a doubt. It was docks and nettles for us. We had searched for such a place all over East Anglia, pursuing his urge to create a proper landscape garden.

We bought Columbine Hall in Suffolk in 1993 and I can honestly say, apart from a single, diseased Iceberg rose in the drive's turning circle, there was no garden. However, there were trees such as yew and oak and, better still, a moat more than 10ft deep and, in places, more than 30ft wide. It was this that produced the first design problem as we tried to make some plans. The moat surrounds an acre of land, including the house, which, jettied, stands directly on the water. We had, effectively, a walled garden with no walls. What to do?

> *"What is clever about the garden is that it has a series of uncluttered spaces defined by hornbeam hedges. These are not outdoor rooms, for they allow movement through generous openings, glimpses into other parts of the garden and views out to the countryside."*
>
> *The Good Gardens Guide*, 2010-11

Our answer was to consult George Carter, a high-profile garden designer with numerous Chelsea gold medals who lives in Norfolk and therefore understood the terrain. (Suffolk is one of the driest counties in Britain, has no stone other than flint and is alkaline with patches of clay.) He's known for his modern take on 17th-century formal garden design and avoidance of fancy planting schemes. In a book on his own garden, he says he has tried to make colour 'subservient to everything else'.

Apart from telling us to treat the moat like a giant ha-ha – obvious, really – he brought in JCBs to level the land inside the moat, known as a platform. We changed a gently sloping site into a series or formal, level courtyards, in one place creating the 'hornbeam room', an area with high hedges that makes the highly jumbled footprint of the house symmetrical. 'I devised several small garden compartments to echo the maze-like interior of a medieval house,' he wrote.

He left the planting to us and, because we like to keep things understated, we decided against flowing herbaceous borders or massed shrubberies. For spring, we've planted the white naturalised tulips Triumphator and Spring Green under columns of pleached limes and, in summer, eight rectangular beds planted with square blocks of plants come into their own. The nursery that advised us said it should 'look like a 1960s man's tie'.

We have squares of box bushes for weight along with *Lavandula* Hidcote, *Geranium* Johnson's Blue, *Allium* Schubertii, *Liriope muscari*,

RIGHT The Parterre planted like a 1960s man's tie. Obelisks to a George Carter design.

COLUMBINE HALL

THE GARDEN 39

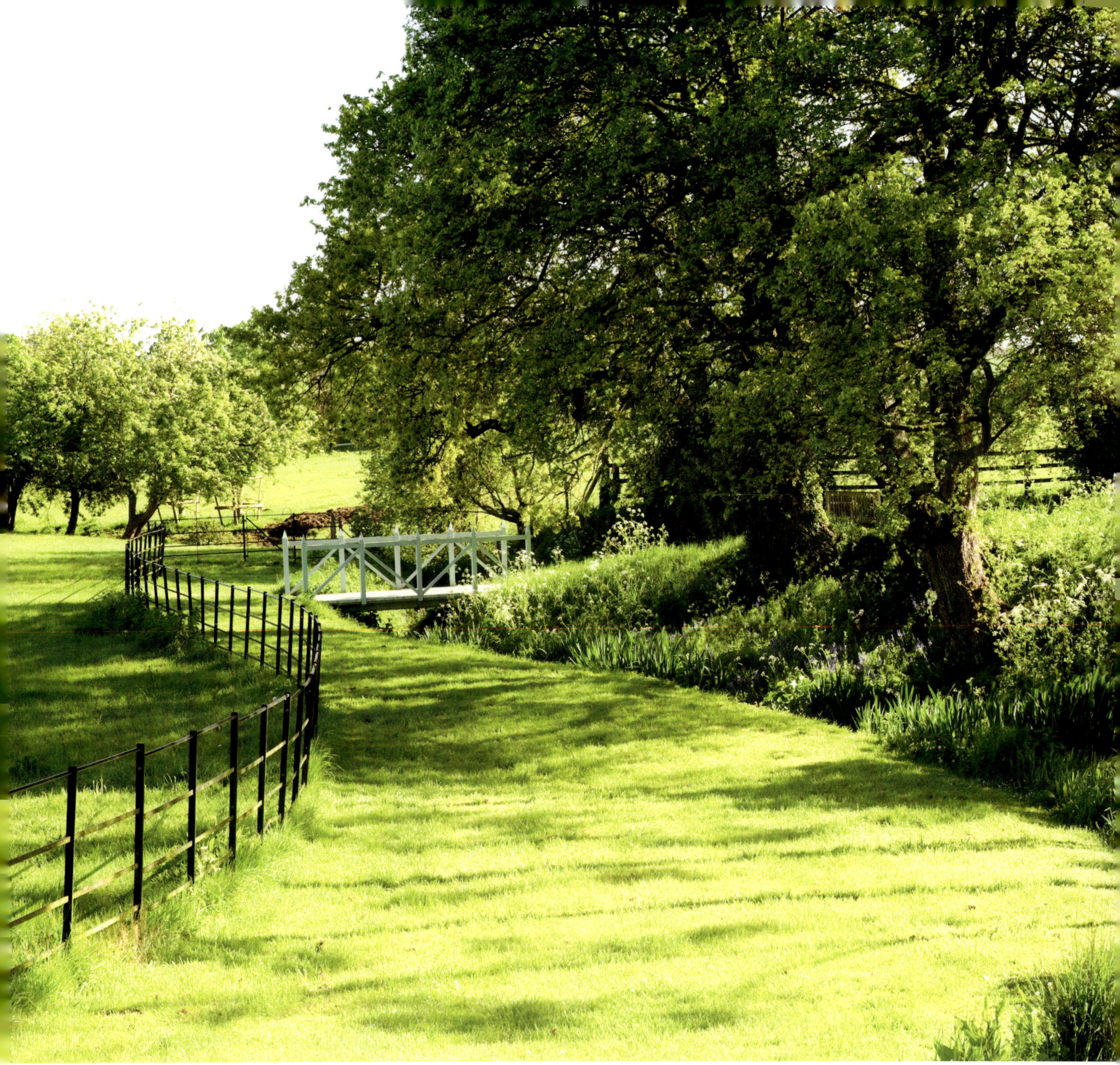

LEFT Iron railings divide a garden walk from the Park.

irises and *Alchemilla mollis*, *Vitis vinifera* Purpurea grapevines climb up six painted obelisks. Nearer the house, we let rip with dark tulips such as Queen of Night, Black Parrot along with Recreado and Estella Rijnveld mixed with lots of alliums, especially *Allium christophii* and *A. sphaero-cephalum*. All are entangled with bronze fennel, which, in early spring, looks like small foxes' tails, but, by July, grows high enough to create an outdoor net curtain to keep prying eyes away.

We leave the moat banks wild: one year, after repairs to its crumbling sides that involved a load of topsoil, we had a splendid and unexpected display of poppies both wild and cultivated. There's always a froth of cow parsley, white and pink valerian and more bronze fennel, which seeds wildly everywhere.

As well as being labour saving – it gets cut once a year, in late summer – it encourages wildlife. We have, around the moat, mallards and Canada geese, kingfishers, green and spotted woodpeckers, goldfinches and innumerable tits. A heron visits to spear the roach that swim in the water. There are reed mace and more yellow-flowered flag irises at the edges.

The whole amounts to 29 acres, of which 24 are landscaped as a park with views down gentle slopes into the countryside beyond. We have carefully included other people's land in our vistas and our fields are let to a neighbouring farmer, who grazes beautiful Red Poll cattle on them. The planting outside the moat is determinedly informal, but, everywhere, we've tried to underpin the wildness with a formal framework: avenues of paired holm oaks and paths of short grass emphasising the vistas.

One area was planted as an orchard, with advice from John Rogers of Secret Gardens. We have walnut trees given to us by a visitor to our open garden day and there are medlars, mulberries, cherries, pears and apples. At the other side of the moat making a connection with this orchard, are two Vranja quinces. The whole is filled with blossom each spring.

THE GARDEN   41

LEFT Wild garlic flowers in the Bog Garden.
OPPOSITE The south-west side of the house with the Herb Garden in the foreground.

I suppose we have been influenced by Italian gardens, especially La Gamberaia outside Florence, where the designers have tried to have a bit of everything in a few acres. Thus, we have a small wilderness of native trees, a shady walk, three classical water spouts and beds with lupins, Welsh poppies and buddleia for the butterflies, all of which seed as they please.

We have wisteria and vines climbing the walls and figs against them. One of the latter is a cutting from the fig tree planted at Lambeth Palace by the last Roman Catholic Archbishop of Canterbury, Cardinal Pole. It came from the Museum of Garden History and they say it's a White Marseilles fig, planted in 1555.

Of course, there's a bog garden, with a stream and small waterfall we created, that's planted with massed ferns, bamboos and, in spring, masses of white-flowering wild garlic (good for soup), bluebells, wild flag and Florentine irises. To cross the stream, there are three bridges copied, like the obelisks, from George's designs and painted in Farrow & Ball's G7 (which was used by Churchill at Chartwell).

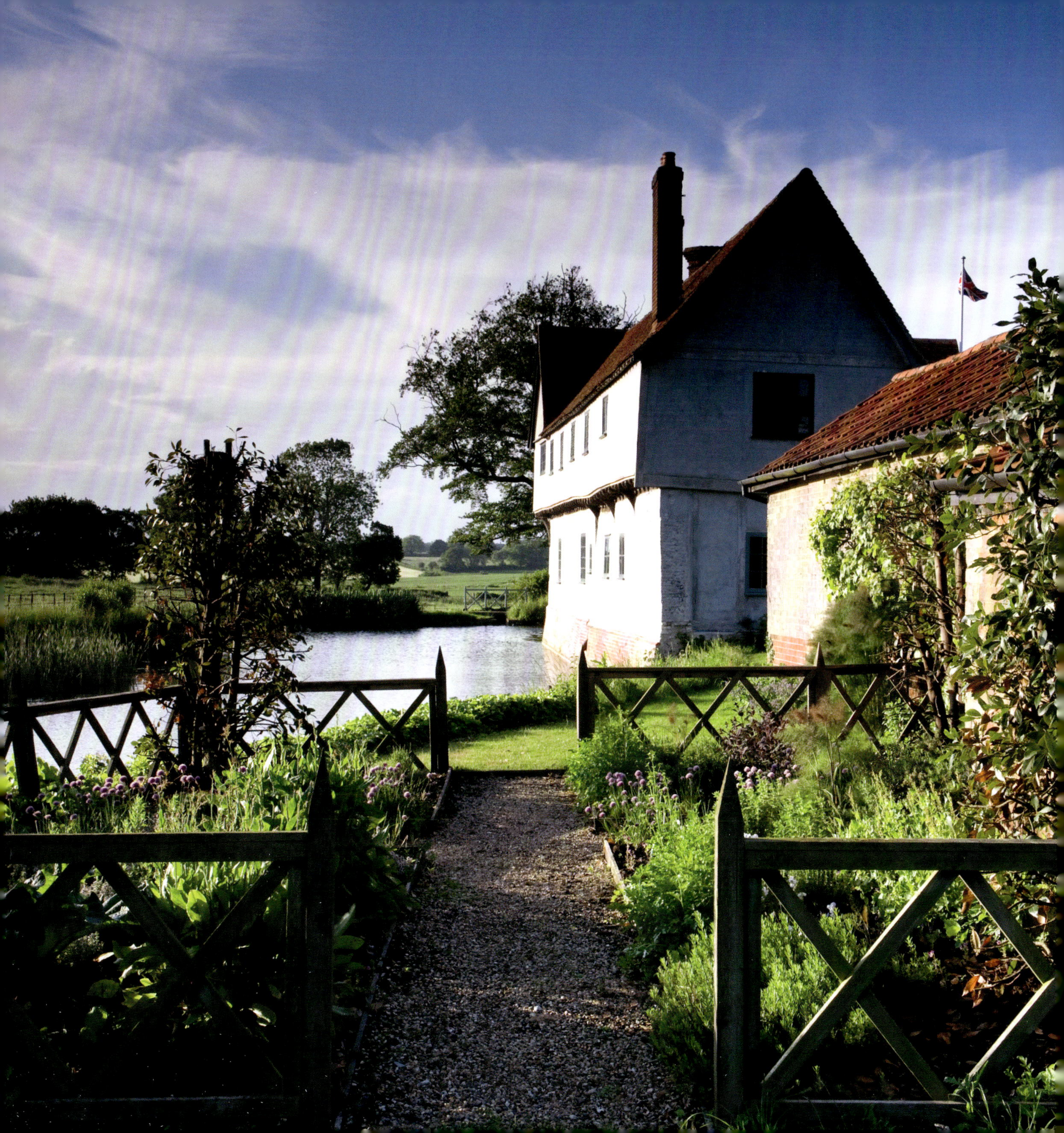

RIGHT The Walled Garden with the black-painted Gig House cottage beyond.

The same design is used to surround a small herb garden on the platform beside the moat. At each corner, we've planted a columnar bay tree. There's a row of flowering chives and more showy alliums, thyme picked wild in Italy, more lavender and statuesque artichokes, which we use to make architectural statements. At one side, I've planted mint in a bed known as the Royal Mint bed because we created it during the week of Prince William's marriage to Kate Middleton.

Then, there's the walled garden. This is inspired by that at Chateau de Bosmelet in Normandy and is the creation of Kate Elliott, our head gardener, who came to Columbine straight from school more than 20 years ago. It has four colour-themed beds filled with kales such as Cavolo Nero and Redbor, with courgettes, shallots and borlotti beans, the whole surrounded by marigolds and nasturtiums.

Here we can indulge in colour, so there are old roses climbing the walls: William Lobb, Charles de Mills, Camaieux and Comptesse de Murinais. The black-painted barn at the end has two white climbing roses on each side of the door, Mme Plantier and Boule de Neige.

In this complex of black-painted buildings, created from old barns, cart sheds and stables, we have been able to take advantage of the black background to plant climbers such as wisteria and more vines, to set Versailles tubs filled with bamboo symmetrically by doorways and arches and let golden hops writhe among the gateposts. A holiday cottage converted from a stable has its own small garden surrounded with a hawthorn hedge and planted with nepeta, lavender and thyme.

To create an understated rural space needs discipline, so we try to deny any urge to floss the garden up. Many visitors to the garden from as far afield as America and Japan praise its peaceful atmosphere. Like all gardens, the peace is only achieved as a result of frenetic self-control.

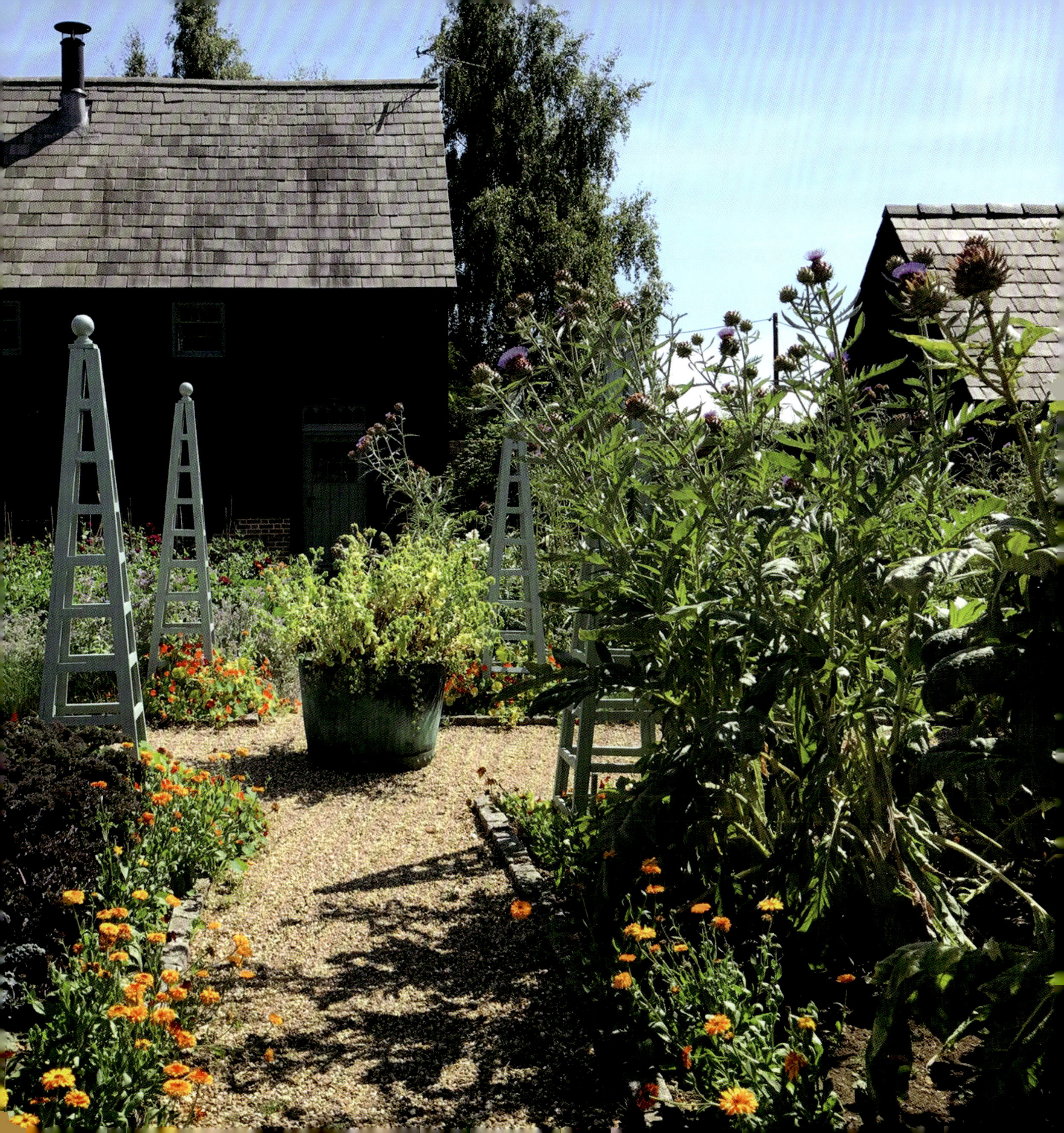

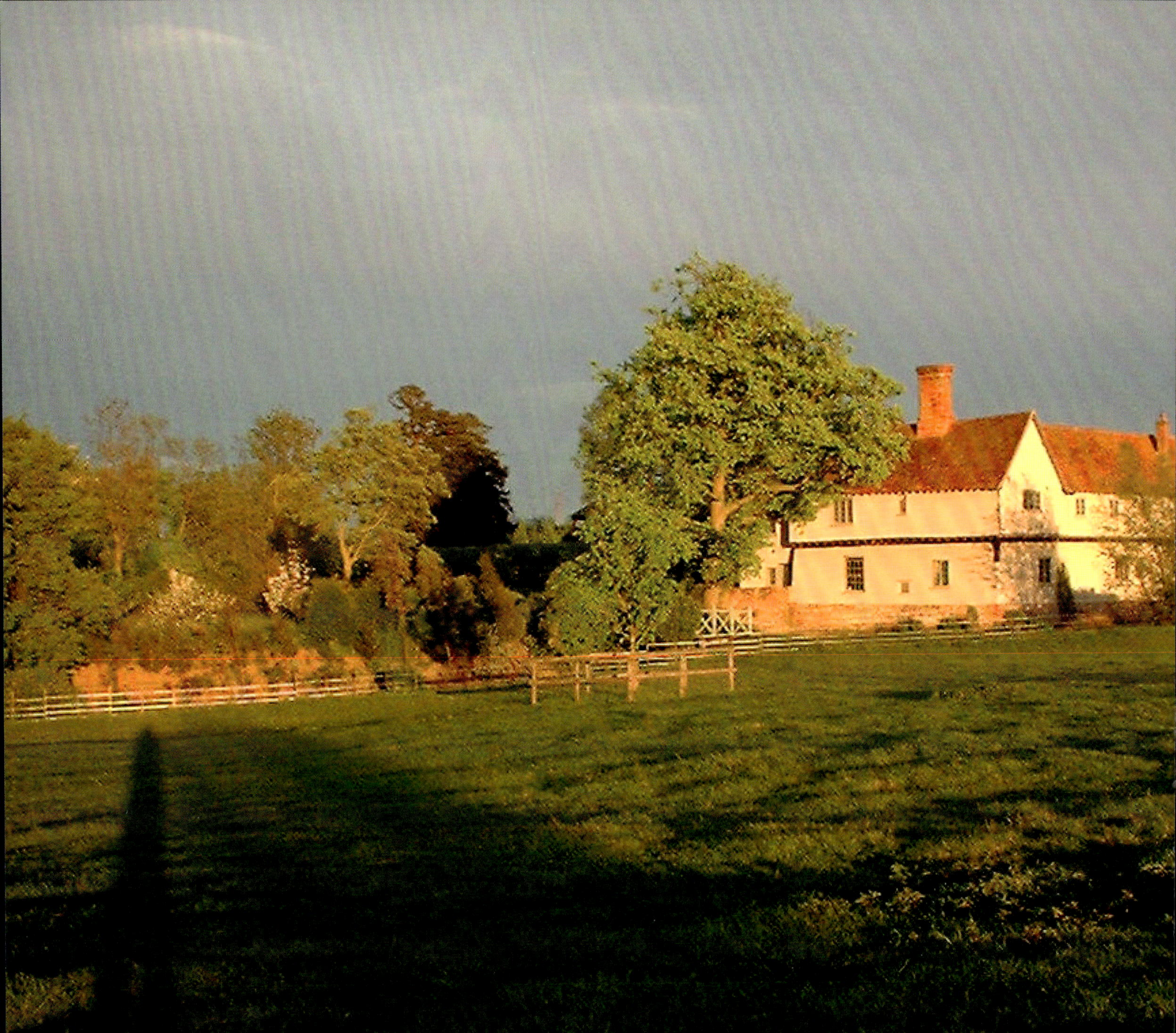

Chapter Four

The Medieval Manor

"Surrounded by rich green meadows and old trees, there is still much that suggests an imparkment of the fifteenth century, and within this a moated manor house which, in slowly declining from its former status, has preserved an atmosphere of indefinable timelessness"

Eric Sandon, *Suffolk Houses*, 1977

Owners of Columbine Hall 1242–1557

FEUDAL OVERLORDS

Philip de Columbers
of Nether Stowey, Somerset. Held manor of Battisford 1242 and, in that capacity, was feudal overlord of Thorney Columbers (Columbine Hall).
d. 1257

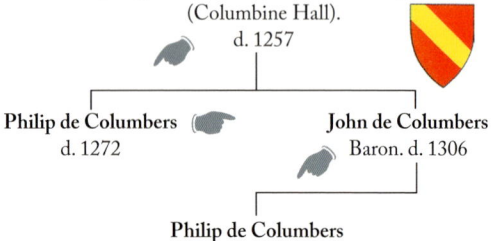

Philip de Columbers
d. 1272

John de Columbers
Baron. d. 1306

Philip de Columbers
Baron 1314. Sold the Manor of Battisford 1317.
Died childless 1342.

John Salmon, Bishop of Norwich
Bought the Manor of Battisford (and feudal overlordship of Columbine Hall) in 1317. It remained with the Bishops of Norwich until the dissolution of the monasteries, c1540.

Henry VIII
Acquired the overlordship on seizing the monasteries.
It has since remained with the Crown.

RESIDENT LORDS OF THE MANOR

John de Hotot
Held the manor of Thorney Columbers (Columbine Hall) under the de Columbers family, 1242

John de Hotot
Held the manor, 1326
Taxed 3/6d in Thorney, 1327

Robert le Hotot
d. c1326

Robert Hotot
A prominent justice in Suffolk 1381-99.
Probable builder of the present Columbine Hall, c1390
d. by 1402

John Hotoft
of Columbine Hall
d. c1452

Robert Hotoft
of Columbine Hall. Married Joan, daughter of John Fitz-Ralph Esq. of Pebmarsh, Essex. He died 1469.

John Hotoft
of Columbine Hall. d. by 1516

Sir James Tyrrell of Gipping
Alleged murderer of the Princes in the Tower (though this is disputed). Beheaded 1502.

James Tyrrell ....married............ **Anne Hotoft**
d. c1539   Heiress of Columbine Hall
                                                  d. c1534

John Tyrrell
of Columbine Hall

Thomas Tyrrell
of Columbine Hall.
Lost the estate through a foreclosed mortgage, 1557

East Anglia has more moated sites than any other county in England perhaps because of its flat land and clay soil. Some were for defence, others to provide a supply of fish – or water – and some simply for show. The moat at Columbine Hall is unusually deep (12 feet in places) which implies defence, though the date of its construction is unknown. In the ninth century the Vikings in their longships were raiding England's eastern counties, finally subduing the Saxon inhabitants and imposing Danish rule. Hollingsworth in his *History of Stowmarket* (1844) refers to a big battle at a place called Stonebridge on the River Gipping, just below Columbine Hall where sword blades, spear heads, pieces of armour and "horses' shoes of great breadth" were unearthed. Traces of an entrenchment, only just still visible from the air, in Columbine Hall's meadow, Park Hill, are said to be where the Danes encamped and from which they mounted an attack on whatever structure – perhaps of wood – that stood within the moated enclosure.

From 1066 William I, having defeated King Harold at Hastings, ruled England and handed out land to his Norman knights. The Domesday Book

ABOVE LEFT Two types of medieval joint. The lower one is a splayed scarf joint with undersquinted abutment.
ABOVE RIGHT Early wall painting in one of the bedrooms.
PREVIOUS PAGES Seen from the West, Columbine Hall is lit by the setting sun.

THE MEDIEVAL MANOR

Columbers

records that in 1086: "King William holds Thorney which King Edward [the Confessor] held as one manor and as 5 carucates of land". Over the next hundred and fifty years Thorney was subdivided into separate manors, one of which became known (after its feudal overlords) as Thorney Columbers. In 1242 Philip de Columbers of Nether Stowey in Wiltshire, a member of a Norman family from Colombières, near Bayeux, held the manor of Battisford in Suffolk of which Thorney Columbers was a dependency. Philip's son and grandson were each successively summoned to parliament as barons.

The resident lord of Thorney Columbers manor, however, in 1242 was John de Hotot (possibly from Huttoft in Lincolnshire) and his descendants, sometimes Hotost or Hotoft, continued to hold the manor for the next three hundred years. Another John de Hotot held the manor in 1327, being taxed three shillings and sixpence in Thorney that year. His successor Robert le Hotot and his wife Alice were staking a claim to the neighbouring manor of Thorney Clements in the 1330s and '40s.

Robert died in about 1346 and was succeeded by his son, another Robert. Two years later The Black Death swept across England with devastating effect. A third of the population perished. The peasants who remained and whose status required them to work without pay, on the country's manorial lands, found that their services were now in short supply. They began to demand rights and their pent-up resentment finally erupted in the Peasants' Revolt in 1381. They ransacked the manor houses and burnt the manorial rolls in a gesture of defiance against the feudal system that had oppressed them for so long – probably why hardly any of the Columbine Hall manorial records from before that date have survived.

By 1377 the Thorney Columbers manor was held by John's son Robert Hotot. He was a prominent justice in Suffolk from 1381, the year of the Peasants' Revolt, and was no doubt kept busy with its aftermath which may not have endeared him to the populace. He was active in county affairs

ABOVE A Charles II chair in front of a 14th-century doorway.
LEFT A blocked-up medieval window. The groove in the beam above was for sliding wood shutters.

THE MEDIEVAL MANOR 51

MEDIEVAL RAFTER TYPES

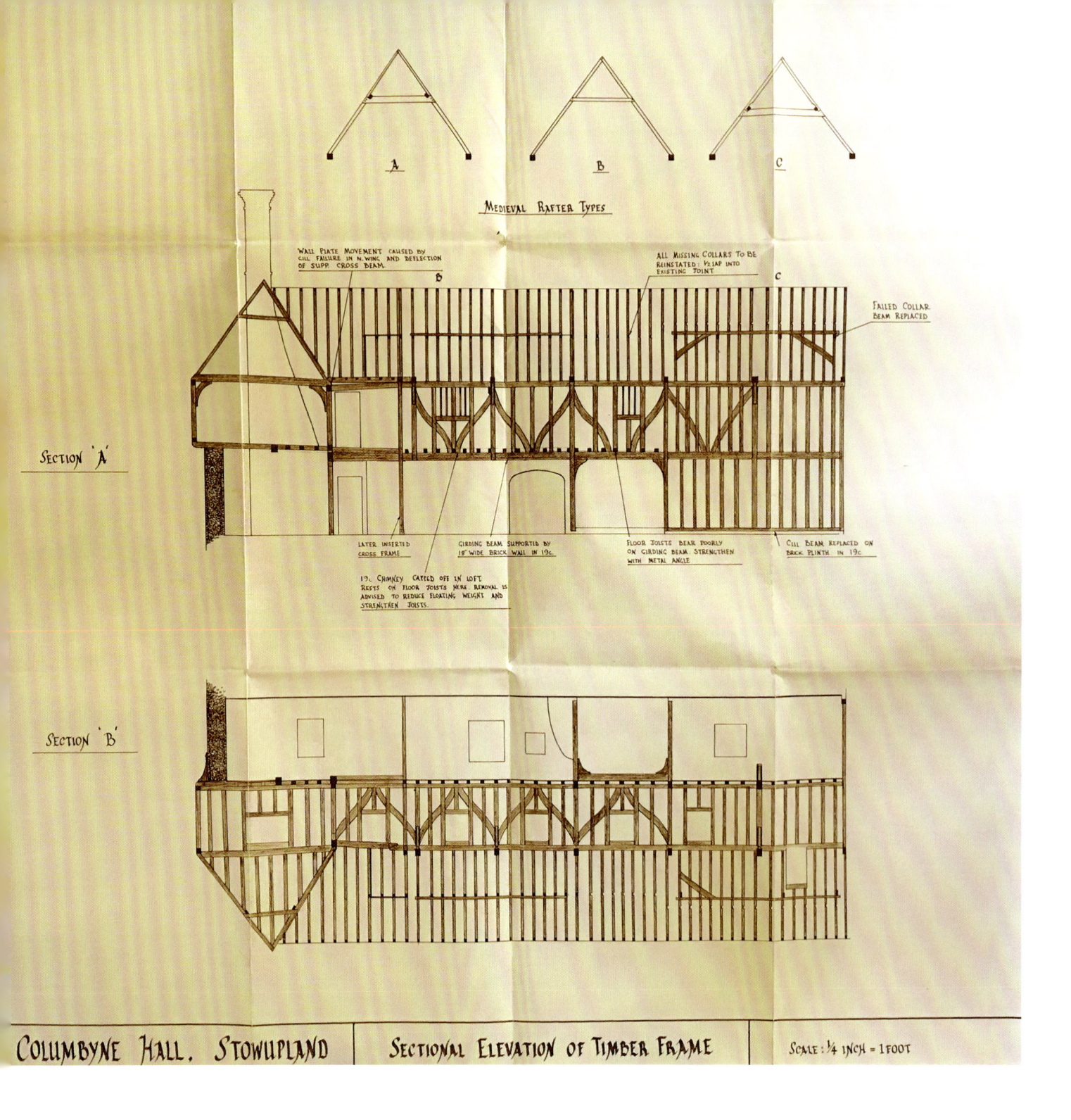

A B C

Section 'A'

- Wall plate movement caused by cill failure in N. wing and deflection of supp. cross beam.
- All missing collars to be reinstated: ½ lap into existing joint
- Failed collar beam replaced
- Later inserted cross frame
- Girding beam supported by 18" wide brick wall in 19c.
- 19c. chimney carried off in loft rests on floor joists here removal is advised to reduce floating weight and strengthen joists.
- Floor joists bear poorly on girding beam strengthen with metal angle
- Cill beam replaced on brick plinth in 19c.

Section 'B'

COLUMBYNE HALL. STOWUPLAND — SECTIONAL ELEVATION OF TIMBER FRAME — SCALE: ¼ INCH = 1 FOOT

52 COLUMBINE HALL

Hotot

OPPOSITE Melvyn Smith's drawing of the timber frame of the west wing.

until his death in about 1402. It was probably he who, conscious of his status, replaced his old manor house with a new and grander Columbine Hall which he sited picturesquely, like some of the chateaux of France and according to the latest fashion, right on the edge of the water rather than in the middle of his moated site. The edges of the moat supporting the house were reinforced with new foundations; hence the ground floor walls on the moat side are of flint while the upper timber-framed storey is jettied out to enhance the dramatic effect. The inner banks of the moat were protected by a massive wall of flint and rubble, the remains of which can still be seen lying partly under water on the north and east side. The eastern section was said to be still standing seven to eight feet above water level (though not above ground level) in the 1930s (East Anglian Magazine, May 1937).

The close-studded timber framing of the upper storey was evidently intended to be shown with plastering in between. It had been rendered over in modern times with white-painted cement and when we had the badly-cracked cement render removed, we toyed with exposing the timber frame to reveal Robert Hotot's original elevation once more. English Heritage were prepared to agree but the timbers were too badly weathered to produce anything but a hotch-potch effect so we had it re-rendered with lime plaster.

Only a fragment of Robert Hotot's prestigious medieval manor house remains today. The main entrance was via a bridge across the moat through an archway (now blocked up) through the west range of Columbine Hall. When we had the moat dredged in 1994 some blackened oak timbers, presumably the remnants of the old bridge, were found in the mud (where they still remain). This west range extended further south than it does today. The old approach, across the bridge and through the arch, is likely to have come into a courtyard with the principal hall (which has long since disappeared) before it. The present west wing was therefore a gatehouse range with the present north wing adjoining it at right angles. The west wing could, at its southern end, have had a return wing going to the east, forming a quadrangle with the main hall forming the eastern side of the square. But this is all conjecture.

Robert Hotot was succeeded in 1402 by his son John whose own son, another Robert, married Joan, a daughter of John Fitz-Ralph esquire of Pebmarsh, Essex, and was lord of the Columbine Hall manor until his own death in 1469. John Hotoft, Robert II's son was the last of the Hotoft male line to hold the manor and on his death in 1516 the estate was inherited by his daughter Anne.

The Thorney Columbers manorial records are now in the Suffolk Record Office in Ipswich. They have been described by Dr Nicholas Amor, chairman of the Suffolk Institute of Archaeology and History, as "one of the best runs of court rolls for any manor of late medieval Suffolk". Sixty rolls cover the period 1400 to 1510. They report in detail the doings of the manor court which imposed fines on those who had trespassed, or allowed their animals to stray on the lord's land. In 1467 two Stowmarket men were found guilty of breaking and entering with staffs and daggers the premises of Robert Hotot Esquire and poaching the perch, tench and roach in his waters.

Anne Hotoft, the heiress, married a neighbour, James Tyrrell, a younger son of Sir James Tyrrell of Gipping Hall, Richard III's Master of the Horse, and the man who is supposed to have murdered the princes in the Tower at the behest, depending on your viewpoint, of either Richard III or Henry VII. On showing a group of visitors round Columbine Hall one day, we casually referred to Richard as being responsible. We were met with a stony silence; we then remembered that the group we were addressing was the Richard III Society. Sir James Tyrrell was beheaded for treason in 1502 and the charming small chapel at Gipping (in which a service is still conducted on the first Sunday of every month) was built to honour his memory and, it is supposed, to atone for his misdeeds.

Tyrrell

54 COLUMBINE HALL

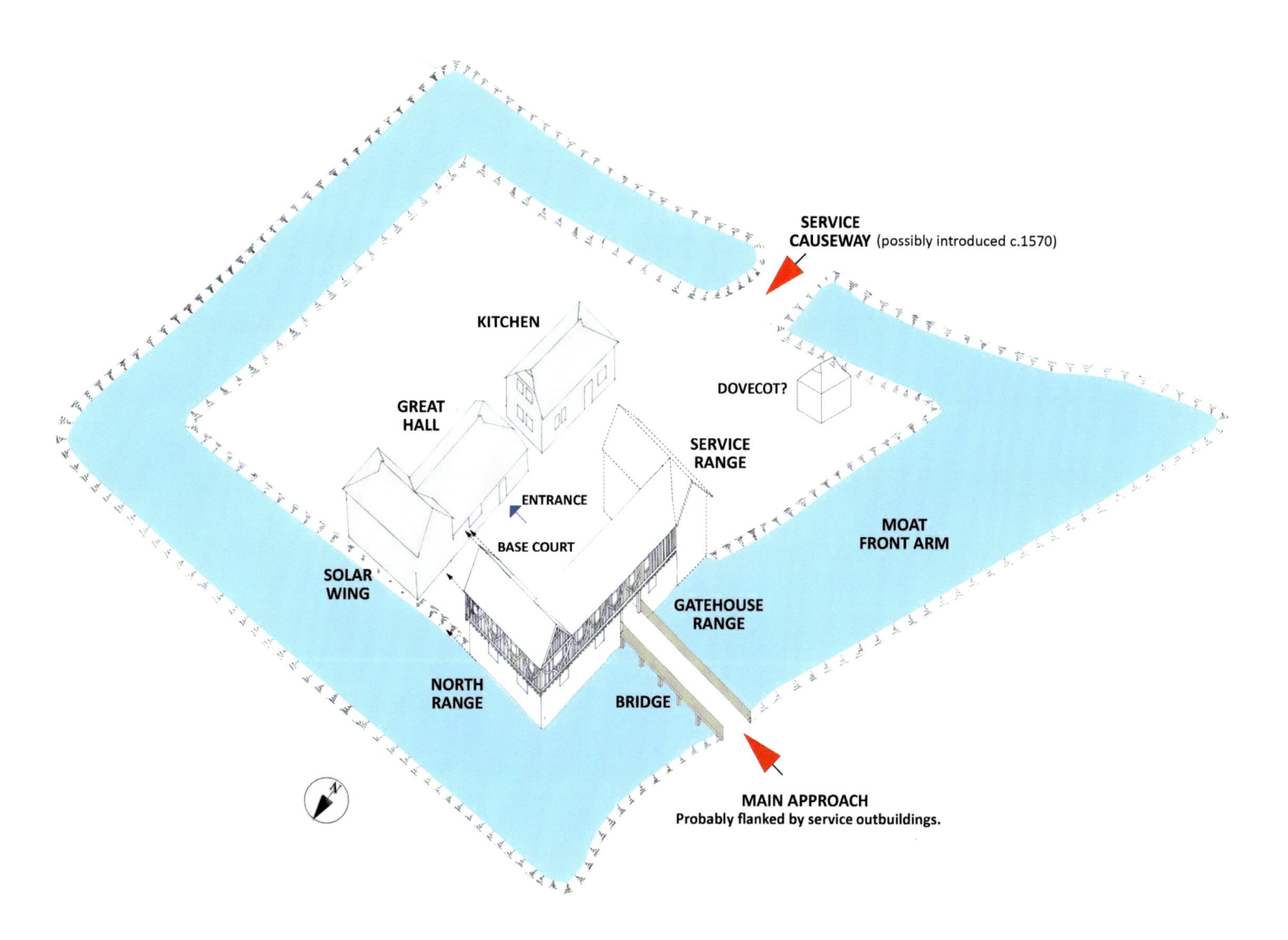

ABOVE A reconstruction of what Columbine Hall probably looked like in medieval times. What remains today is the west and north wings plus the George IV wing at the eastern side.

His son's marriage brought Columbine Hall into the Tyrrell family and James and Anne's grandson, Thomas, was in possession of the manor in Elizabeth I's reign. But the family evidently fell on hard times for in 1557 Thomas Tyrrell, through a foreclosed mortgage, lost the manor that his ancestors had owned for 300 years. The mortgagee was a London merchant, Thomas Stanbridge, who became the new owner – to the lasting resentment of the Tyrrells.

THE MEDIEVAL MANOR 55

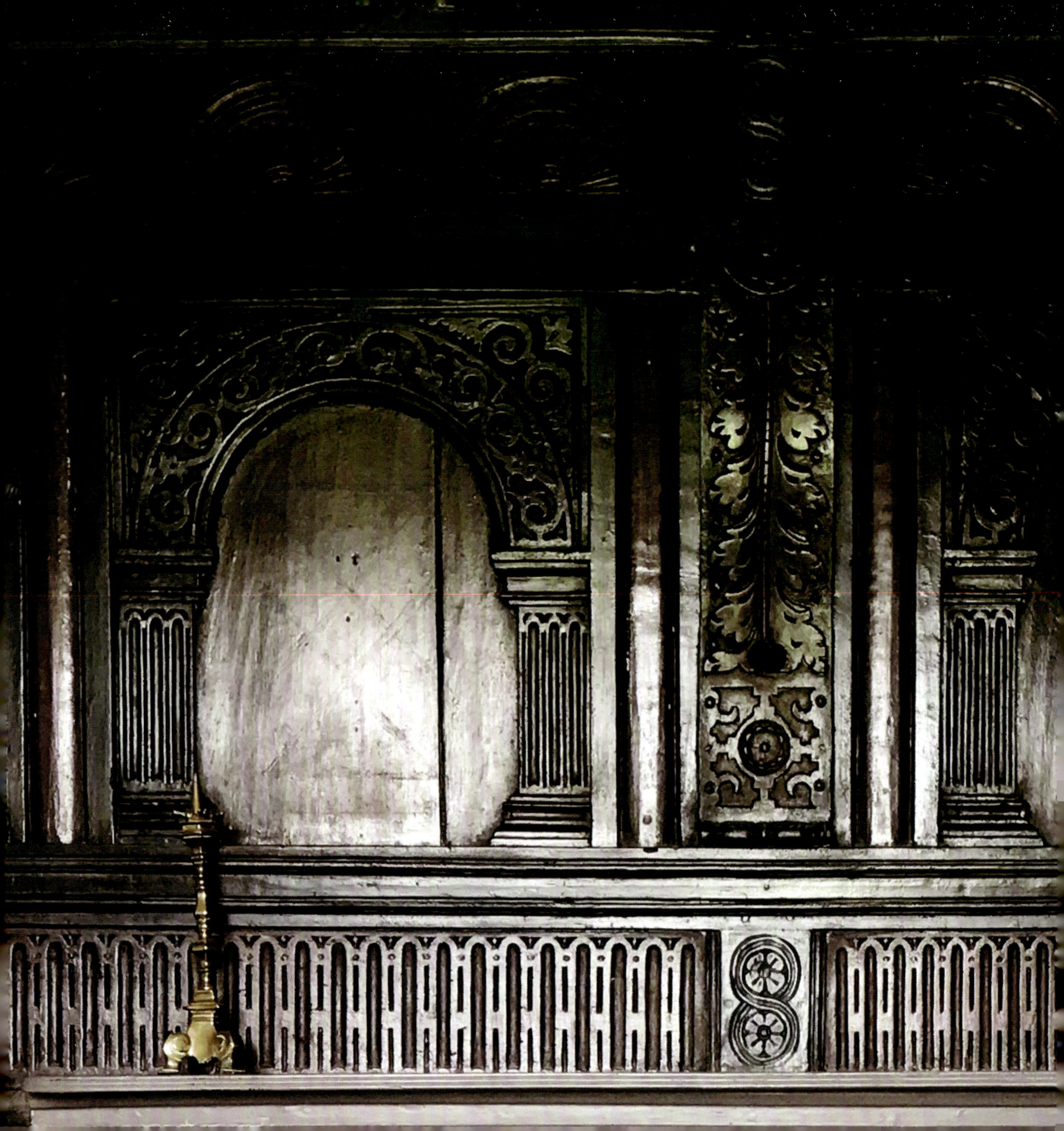

Chapter Five

A Grand Time

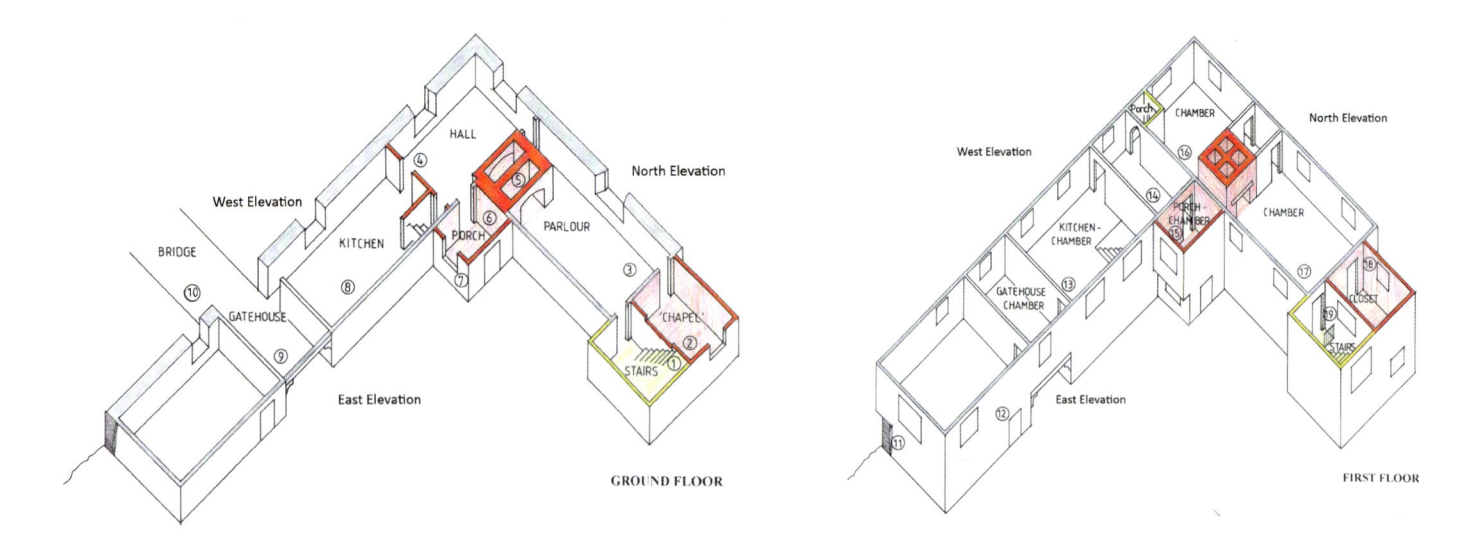

ABOVE An architectural historian's conjectural view of the building in the medieval and Tudor period.
PREVIOUS PAGES The overmantel in the north west chamber dates from the time of Sir John Poley.

Carey

In 1559, two years after Thomas Stanbridge had acquired Columbine Hall, he sold it on to John Gardiner, gent, of London, who made alterations to his new home. It may have been he who demolished what was left of the great hall and the extremities of the north and west wings of the Hotoft era. Perhaps they had fallen into disrepair under the Tyrrells. The house that Gardiner remodelled survives more or less intact today. He added a small separate (but now joined to the main house) two-storey building to the north east which has traditionally been referred to as "the chapel". Gardiner was probably responsible for the tall brick chimney stack to serve four hearths and a jettied porch in the north west angle of the courtyard which became the main entrance to his new home. It is now a larder with bathroom above.

But John Gardiner and his wife Agnes (daughter of John Smyth of Cavendish) were harried by legal claims from the former owners. The Tyrrells wanted their property back and, although Thomas Tyrrell had died by 1567, his relatives continued fighting to reinstate the property to his three-year-old daughter and heiress Anne. In 1582, after more than two decades, the matter was finally settled with a payment to the now 18-year-old Anne, leaving Gardiner and his wife to enjoy Columbine Hall in relative peace.

In 1587 John and Agnes Gardiner came to an agreement with Henry Carey, the 1st Baron Hunsdon, as to the future of Columbine Hall. Hunsdon wanted to provide an estate for his younger son William and, in return for a financial payment, it was agreed that the Gardiners would retain the estate for their lives, after which it would go to William Carey.

Owners of Columbine Hall 1557-1730

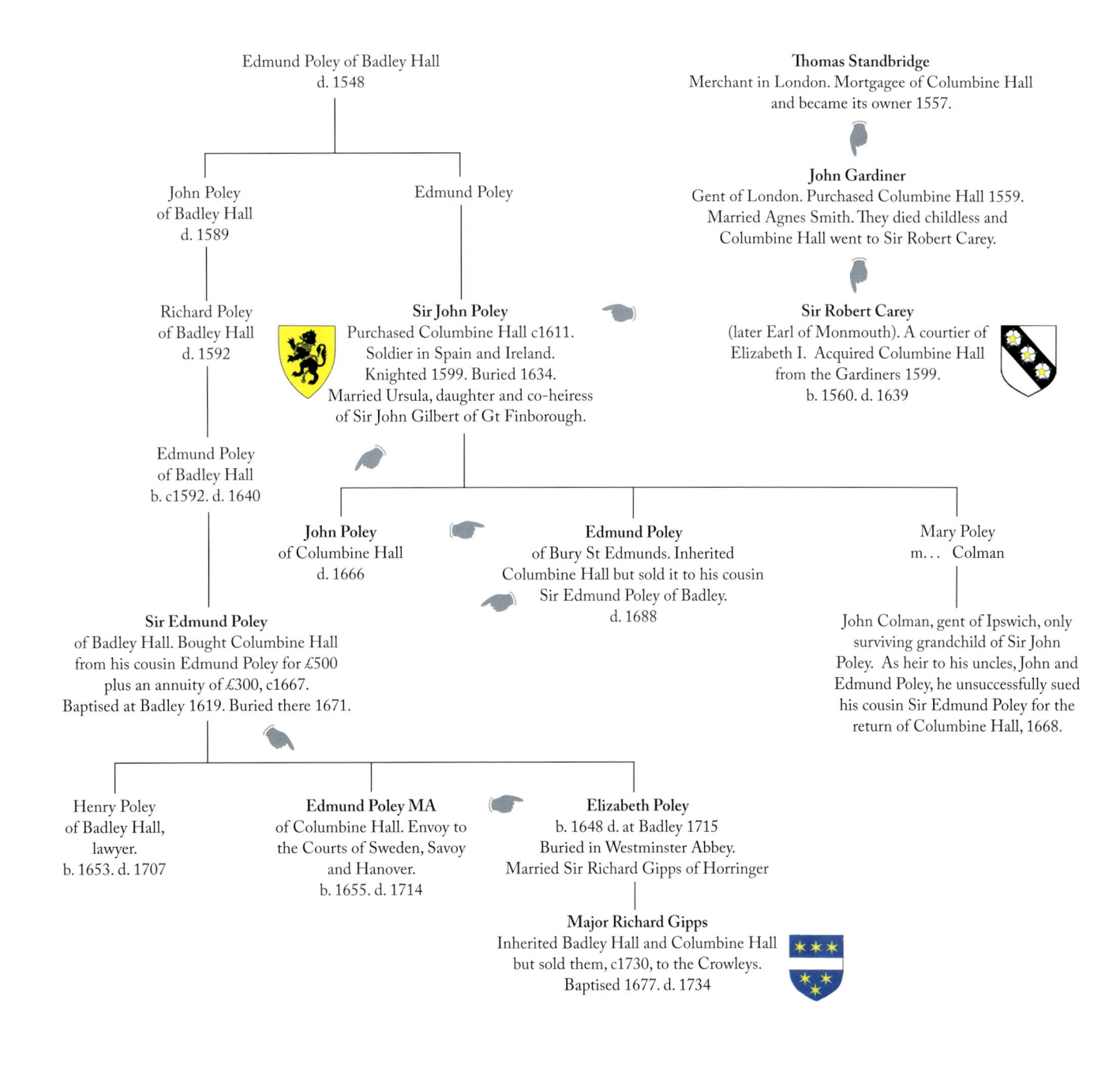

Edmund Poley of Badley Hall
d. 1548

Thomas Standbridge
Merchant in London. Mortgagee of Columbine Hall and became its owner 1557.

John Poley
of Badley Hall
d. 1589

Edmund Poley

John Gardiner
Gent of London. Purchased Columbine Hall 1559. Married Agnes Smith. They died childless and Columbine Hall went to Sir Robert Carey.

Richard Poley
of Badley Hall
d. 1592

Sir John Poley
Purchased Columbine Hall c1611. Soldier in Spain and Ireland. Knighted 1599. Buried 1634. Married Ursula, daughter and co-heiress of Sir John Gilbert of Gt Finborough.

Sir Robert Carey
(later Earl of Monmouth). A courtier of Elizabeth I. Acquired Columbine Hall from the Gardiners 1599.
b. 1560. d. 1639

Edmund Poley
of Badley Hall
b. c1592. d. 1640

John Poley
of Columbine Hall
d. 1666

Edmund Poley
of Bury St Edmunds. Inherited Columbine Hall but sold it to his cousin Sir Edmund Poley of Badley.
d. 1688

Mary Poley
m… Colman

John Colman, gent of Ipswich, only surviving grandchild of Sir John Poley. As heir to his uncles, John and Edmund Poley, he unsuccessfully sued his cousin Sir Edmund Poley for the return of Columbine Hall, 1668.

Sir Edmund Poley
of Badley Hall. Bought Columbine Hall from his cousin Edmund Poley for £500 plus an annuity of £300, c1667. Baptised at Badley 1619. Buried there 1671.

Henry Poley
of Badley Hall,
lawyer.
b. 1653. d. 1707

Edmund Poley MA
of Columbine Hall. Envoy to the Courts of Sweden, Savoy and Hanover.
b. 1655. d. 1714

Elizabeth Poley
b. 1648 d. at Badley 1715
Buried in Westminster Abbey.
Married Sir Richard Gipps of Horringer

Major Richard Gipps
Inherited Badley Hall and Columbine Hall but sold them, c1730, to the Crowleys.
Baptised 1677. d. 1734

The problems that ensued are described in the memoirs of Robert Carey, Lord Hunsdon's tenth son:

OPPOSITE Sir Robert Carey (1560-1639)

> There was an old gentleman in Suffolk that had an old wife, his name was Gardiner. They were childless. This man in recompense for some favour my father had done him (after his own life and his wife's) made an estate of a Lordship of his called Columbine Hall in Suffolk, to my brother William and his heirs male, and for want thereof to me and my heirs male, and for want thereof to my father and his heirs male for ever.
>
> My brother [William] marries, and by fraudulent meanes, privately cuts mee off from the intaile, and by the consent of Gardiner and his wife, makes his own wife a jointure of this Lordship. My brother died without children. Then came it out that this land was given in jointure to his wife. I commenced a suit of law with her, my eldest brother took her part, by reason that if she had prevailed, after her life, the law had cast the land upon him.

John Gardiner was dead by 1596 and his widow then married the ill-fated John Browne of Leiston, whose name appears in various deeds relating to the Columbine Hall manor. John Browne was murdered in 1606. His wife Agnes and the couple's servant Peter were the perpetrators though their motive is unknown. Peter was hanged from the Leiston gibbet and Agnes was burnt, which suggests she was executed as a witch.

Robert Carey, however, after winning his case against his elder brother's wife in the Court of Chancery, duly took possession of Columbine Hall. The Careys were related to the Queen. Lord Hunsdon's mother was Mary, sister of Anne Boleyn, Henry VIII's second wife. This made Hunsdon a first cousin of Queen Elizabeth I. However, the relationship was probably closer because Hunsdon's real father was thought to be the king himself. His mother Mary Boleyn, although married, was "a great whore and more notorious than all others" and was the king's mistress from 1522 to about 1526. Hunsdon was born in 1525.

Sir Robert Carey – he had been knighted in 1591 – was the most distinguished of Columbine Hall's owners. However, his government appointments in Northumberland suggest he is unlikely to have lived at Columbine personally and he leased the manor to Giles Keble, a member of a

COLUMBINE HALL

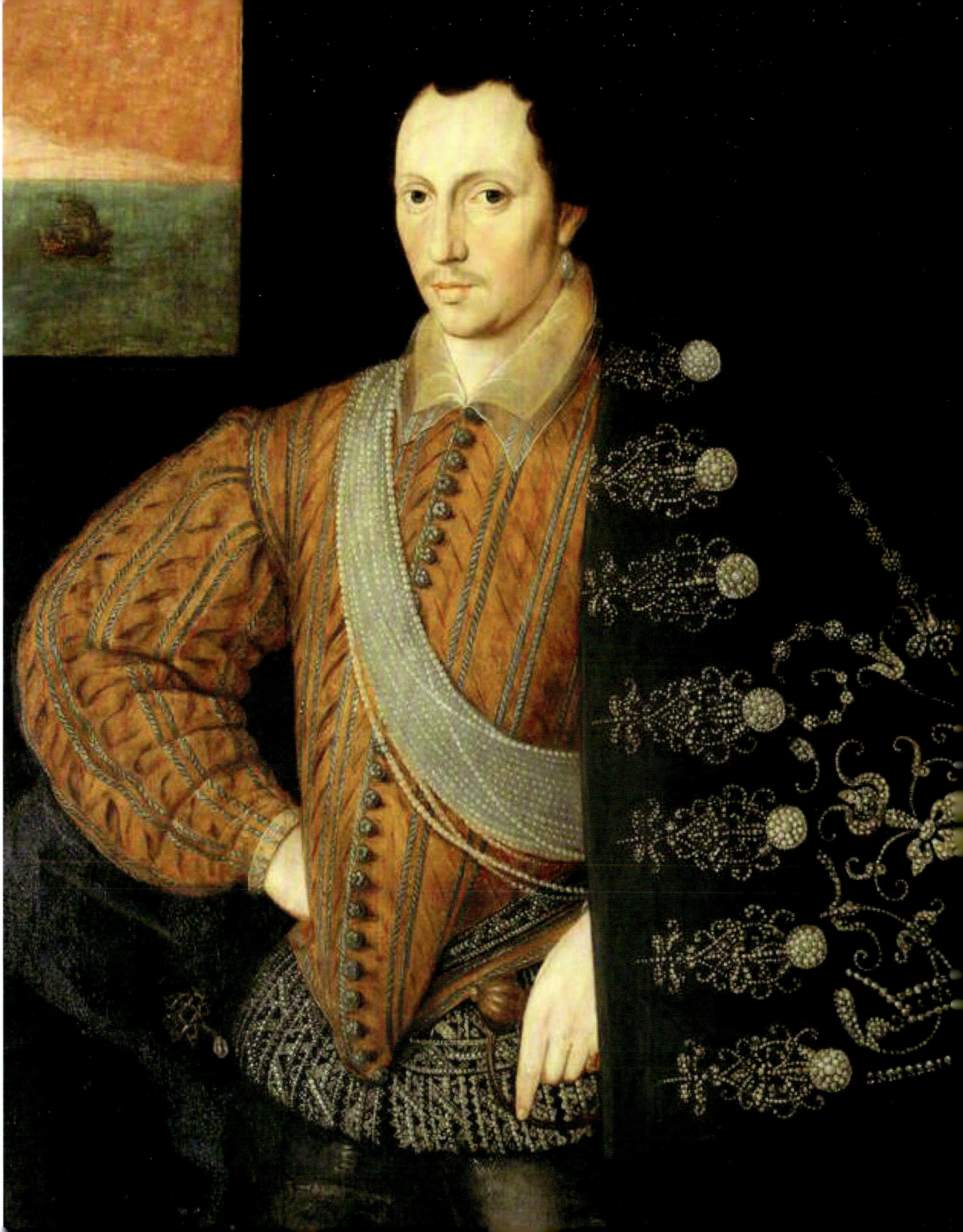

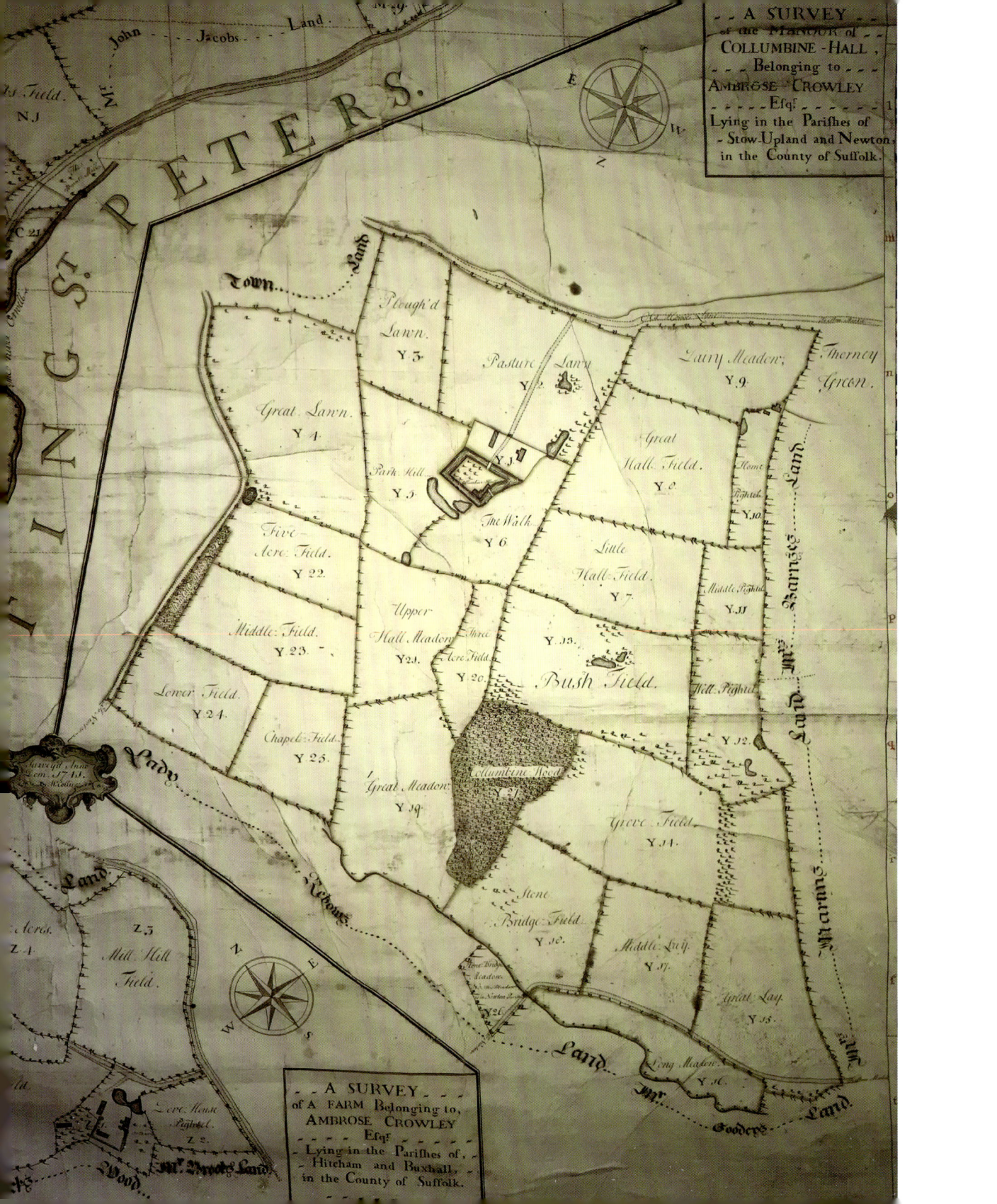

A SURVEY
of the MANOR of
COLLUMBINE-HALL,
Belonging to
AMBROSE CROWLEY Esqr.
Lying in the Parishes of
Stow-Upland and Newton
in the County of Suffolk.

A SURVEY
of A FARM Belonging to
AMBROSE CROWLEY Esqr.
Lying in the Parishes of
Hitcham and Buxhall
in the County of Suffolk.

Mr. John Jacobs Land.

KING ST. PETERS

Town Land

Plough'd Lawn Y3
Pasture Lawn Y2
Dairy Meadow Y9
Thorney Green
Great Lawn Y4
Park Hill Y5
Y1
Great Hall Field Y8
Home Pightel Y10
Five Acre Field Y22
The Walk Y6
Little Hall Field Y7
Middle Pightel Y11
Middle Field Y23
Upper Hall Meadow Y21
Three Acre Field Y20
Y13
Bush Field
Hell Pightel
Lower Field Y24
Y12
Chapel Field Y25
Collumbine Wood Y27
Great Meadow Y19
Grove Field Y14
Stone Bridge Field Y26
Middle Ley Y17
Mill Hill Field Z3
Great Ley Y15
Stone Bridge Meadow
Long Meadow Y16

Surveyd Anno Dom 1743 by W. Collins

Lady

Dove House Pightel Z2
Mr. Brooks Land

Wood

Mr. Goodere Land

Mr. Harvey's Land

OPPOSITE Ambrose Crowley commissioned the cartographer William Collier to survey his estates in Suffolk in 1741. This detail shows the manor of Columbine Hall.

Poley

Stowmarket family of yeomen, for a 15-year term.

Carey was one of Elizabeth I's courtiers (as well as being probably her half-brother). He was present at the queen's deathbed in 1603 and, after a speedy ride to Edinburgh, he was the first to break the news to James VI of Scotland that he had now also become James I of England. Carey became a mentor to the king's eldest boy, later to become Charles I, and was created Earl of Monmouth in 1625.

In 1608 Carey sold Columbine Hall to a retired soldier, Sir John Poley, for £2,600. But first he had to buy out Keble's lease so that Poley could move in with his wife Ursula. Poley had fought in the wars in Spain and Ireland and had been knighted by the Earl of Essex in 1599. He was a descendant of the Poleys of Badley Hall (four miles south of Columbine) where his cousins still lived. He and Ursula, who was daughter and co-heiress of Sir John Gilbert of Great Finborough, settled into Columbine Hall where Sir John presided over the manor court for the next 26 years. He and Ursula were to have six daughters and two sons.

The carved overmantel in the north-west bedroom and its ovolo-moulded window (now blocked up), dates from Sir John Poley's time and it is likely he also installed the oak staircase. Although this dates from the early seventeenth century it has evidently been taken from another house which explains the cobbled-up appearance it has today.

Sir John Poley died in February 1634 and Columbine Hall went to his eldest son John, then aged 18. "And for a further remembrance of my love to him", Sir John had written in his will, "I doe further give unto him my best horse armour and sword to the end he maie remember that it was my cover in battaile".

Ursula, Lady Poley, continued to preside over the manor court until her elder son John came of age. But the dynasty was not to endure beyond his generation. John died without any surviving children in 1666 and his younger brother Edmund inherited the estate. Edmund, too, died without issue a year-and-a-half later by which time Columbine Hall had come into the hands of one of the Badley cousins, Sir Edmund Poley MP of Badley Hall.

Argument about the ownership of Columbine Hall once more came before the courts. John Colman of Ipswich, whose mother had been one of Sir John Poley's daughters, was next of kin and legal heir to his uncles John

A GRAND TIME 63

OPPOSITE Elizabeth Crowley, heiress of Columbine Hall. In 1756 she married the 2nd Earl of Ashburnham. A "swagger" portrait by William Hoare of Bath, who was a founder member of the Royal Academy.

Gipps

Crowley

Ashburnham

and Edmund. He sued Sir Edmund Poley for the return of Columbine Hall, claiming that Sir Edmund had obtained it by nefarious means. He took the case to Chancery where it transpired that his uncle Edmund, a year before his death, had conveyed the estate to Sir Edmund of Badley in return for a down payment of £500 plus an annuity of £300. Colman therefore lost his case and Columbine Hall, for the next 247 years, was to follow the ownership of the Badley Hall estate.

Sir Edmund died in 1671, his widow continuing to live at Badley Hall. The address of his younger son, another Edmund, was given as Columbine Hall in 1684. Edmund became a diplomat and served as envoy to the courts of Sweden, Savoy and Hanover. At one of his postings, at Regensburg, he had little to do and was accused of spending his time "making love to the frauleins". He became the owner of the Poley estates on the death of his elder brother in 1707. Edmund, who never married, was reported to have been "sick and melancholy for a good while, and has had his head much perplexed about religion" when on 16th May 1714 he apparently hanged himself at his chambers in Lincoln's Inn. Another account says he cut his own throat.

His property was left to his sister, Lady Gipps, who only survived for a year after which Badley and Columbine went to her son, Richard, a major in Viscount Ikerrin's Regiment of Dragoons. Richard Gipps had no wish to retain these Suffolk estates so in 1735 he sold them both to the Crowleys of Barking Hall, Suffolk, a family who had made their fortune on Tyneside as iron merchants.

In 1741 Ambrose Crowley commissioned a huge estate map of his new Suffolk properties. This magnificent work, showing all the field names, now hangs above the main staircase at Columbine Hall.

Ambrose, like several previous owners, had no children and when he died in 1754, his property went to his two sisters. When the younger, Elizabeth, was married two years later she had a fortune of £200,000 (nearly £30 million in today's money). Her husband was John, 2nd Earl of Ashburnham, First Lord of the Bedchamber and Groom of the Stole to George III. Columbine Hall, along with Barking and Badley, thus passed into the ownership of the Ashburnham family who already had their estate at Ashburnham in Sussex. Columbine was to be one of the Ashburnhams' many tenanted farms for the next 160 years.

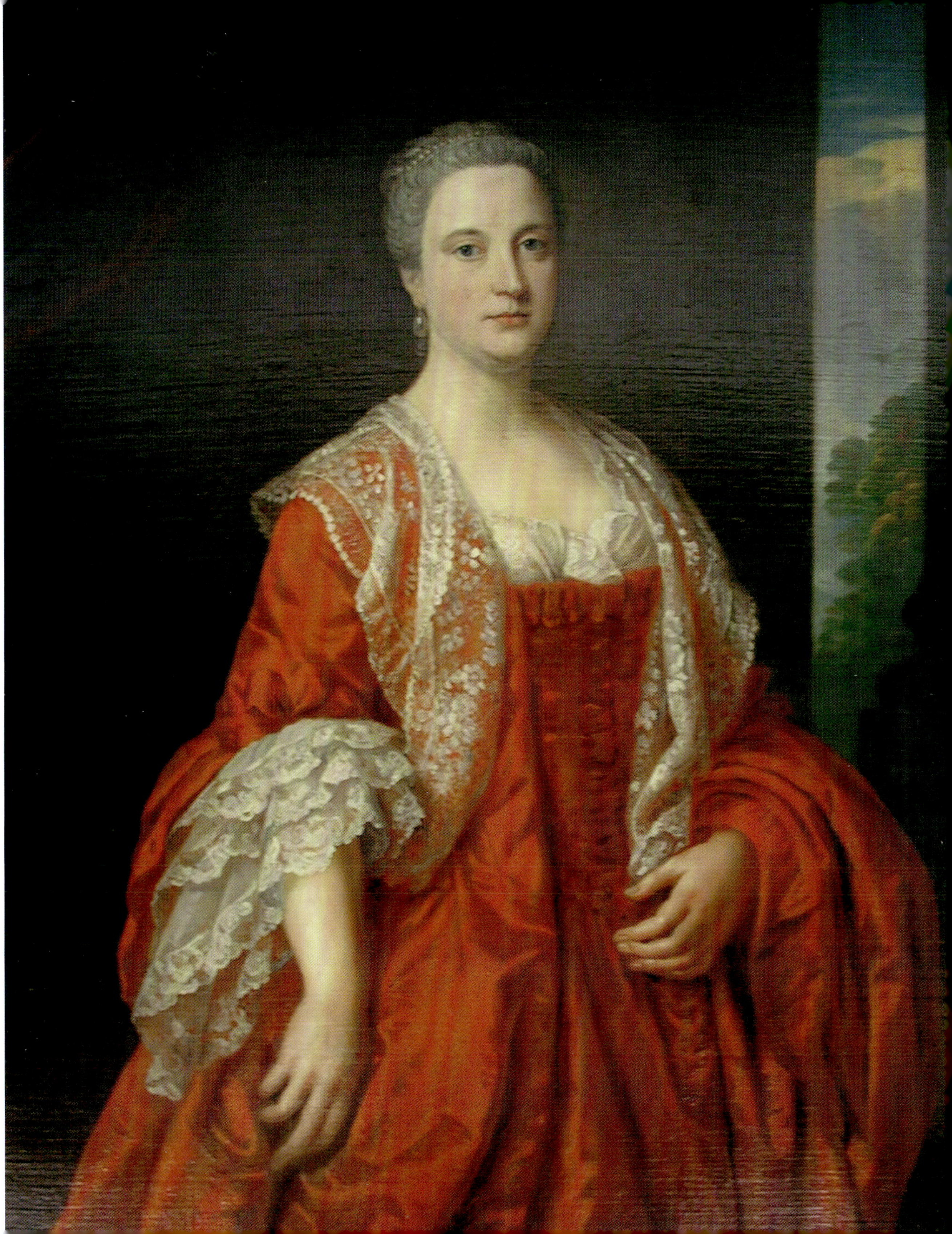

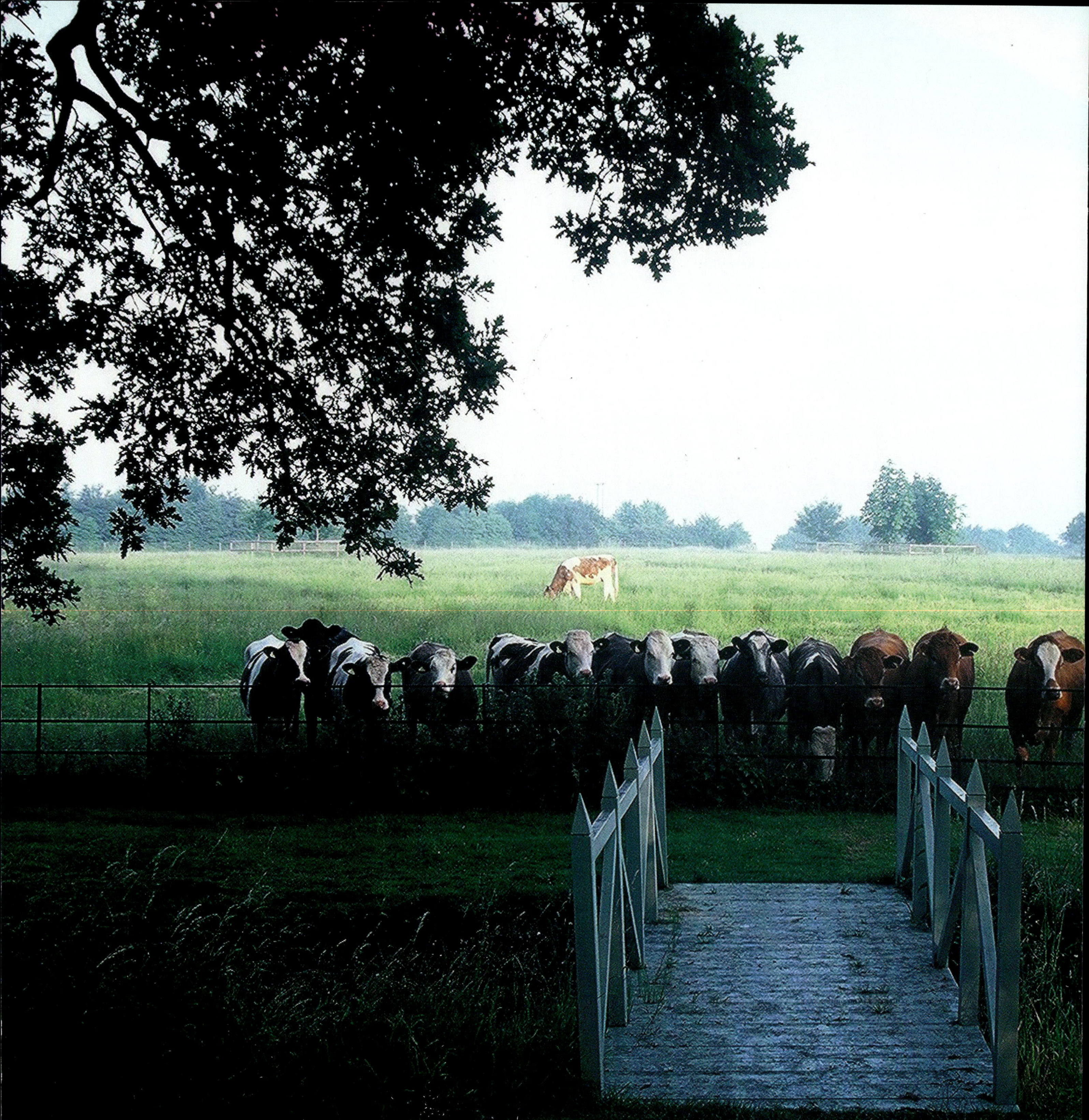

Chapter Six

The Working Farm

After Columbine Hall came into the ownership of the Poleys of Badley in the late 17th century, the property was let to a succession of tenants. By 1695 Thomas Richer was the tenant but by 1715 Major Gipps (whose mother was a Poley) had let Columbine Hall to the Boby family and it has been told how "one old bachelor Boby met with a tragic end; while sleeping in the chimney corner by the open hearth, he fell into the flames and was burnt to death." The tenancy was in the name of Nicholas Boby, a younger son of a family of yeomen who had owned a farm called The Ashes near Stowmarket since the reign of Charles II. Boby died in 1765 and it appears that his grandson, the 25-year-old Nicholas Whaits, took on the tenancy.

In 1804, the then owner, the Earl of Ashburnham, sold Columbine Hall for £11,625 to a William Turner who turned Whaits out and took over the property for himself and his son. Turner enlarged, and to some extent gentrified his new home by adding the south-east brick wing, with drawing room below and a good bedroom above, together with the single-storey entrance hall that leads into it.

But Columbine Hall's revived role as an owner-occupier's residence was to be shortlived. William Turner failed to pay for his purchase so the Earl of Ashburnham took it back and let it once more to the Boby family. Two young brothers, John and Robert Boby, took over the farm in 1835. John was 20 and Robert was 17. They were sons of John Boby senior, owner of The Ashes, and great great grandnephews of Nicholas Boby who had been the Columbine Hall tenant a century before.

By February 1844 the question of selling had cropped up again. The Earl of Ashburnham receiving a letter from his agent, John Kirby Moore,

ABOVE The farming staff at Columbine Hall holding the tools of their trade, c1860. Mr and Mrs Boby are presumably the couple sitting on the right.
OPPOSITE Robert Boby, tenant farmer at Columbine Hall farm from 1835 to 1901.
PREVIOUS PAGES Curious cows belonging to the neighbouring Carter family, who have farmed in Stowupland for six generations, line up in the parkland.

"My Lord, I have been endeavouring to find a purchaser for Columbine Hall but at present have not succeeded."

In August it was still unsold and, although the 26-year-old Robert Boby, by now the sole tenant, had said he would like to buy the 250-acre property, the Earl decided not to sell after all. Robert continued as tenant under the 4th and then the 5th Earl of Ashburnham for the remainder of the century.

In the early days of his tenure there was a spate of arson attacks by discontented farm workers across East Anglia, fuelled by unemployment and low wages. One of the barns at Columbine Hall was burnt down on 26th March 1844. Then on 25th June another large tiled barn and lean-to were set on fire. The culprit was Samuel Jacob, a 28-year-old shepherd who had worked for the Boby brothers and even lived in the house with them. He was convicted and sentenced to transportation for life. On 15th October 1844 he was despatched, along with 249 other convicts, in the ship Hyderabad to the notorious penal settlement on Norfolk Island.

Robert Boby married Elizabeth King in 1845 and they brought up six sons and three daughters at Columbine Hall. His sons used to sit in the house on the window sills fishing in the moat.

THE WORKING FARM 69

OPPOSITE Sale particulars of Columbine Hall, 1914, along with deed of sale to the Potters.

LEFT The Boby family in front of Columbine Hall, c1875
Back row from left: William, Nancy, Frank, Ted, Robert and John.
Sitting: Emily, their parents Robert and Elizabeth, Minnie and Jessie.
In front: Elizabeth and Spencer.

He was an astute farmer, acquiring further land in Stowupland by purchase or lease. By 1881 he was farming 540 acres and employing 22 men and three boys.

Robert Boby retired in 1901 and he and his wife with two unmarried daughters moved to The Chestnuts in Forward Green near Stowupland where he died in 1910 at the age of 92.

The next tenant was Henry Potter, a farmer from Old Newton, who took over Columbine Hall in 1902. His landlord, the 5th Earl of Ashburnham, died in 1913 and a year later his brother Thomas who succeeded him as the 6th (and last) earl put the Columbine Hall farm up for sale. They were divesting themselves of their Suffolk estates. Badley Hall had already been sold and Barking Hall was soon to follow.

Columbine Hall was put up for auction on 30th June 1914 and the 69-year-old Henry Potter bought it at the reserve price of £5,000. After more than two hundred years the farm once more had an owner occupier. Henry

Potter was helped by his two sons, of whom the younger, William, took over the farm when his father died in 1927.

With William Potter, we are now within the realms of living memory. The experiences of the young Brian Hart, a wartime evacuee, are graphically described in Chapter 1.

There was to be a sad ending to the Potters' tenure. During the war, when the enemy were threatening the import of food – especially from America where cargo ships were under attack from German U-boats – efforts to encourage the production of home-grown food were intensified and British farmers were under pressure. The Government decided the Potters' farm was not productive enough and the Ministry of Agriculture (the "War Ag"), took over

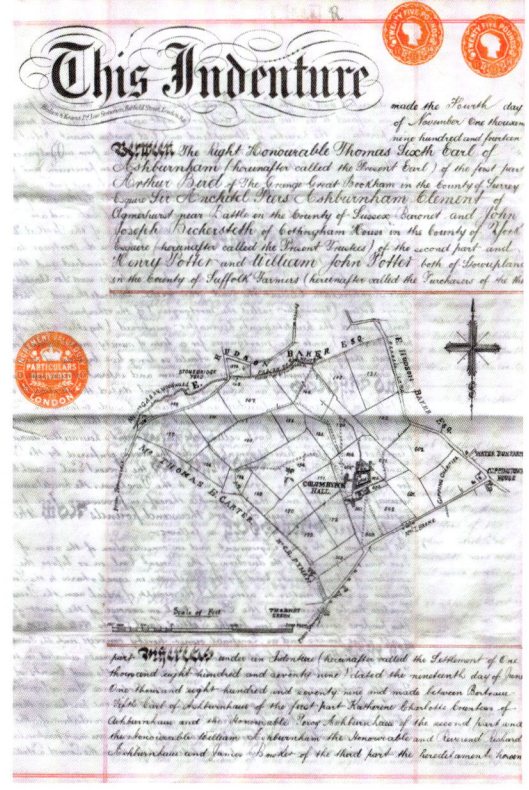

THE WORKING FARM 71

ABOVE On holiday with the Potters, summer 1936. Tillie Wagnall and her son Colin and the pigs.
RIGHT Robert Twitchett and his wife Lillian, surrounded by their family, in front of Columbine Hall, c1947.

the running of the farm. Columbine Hall was compulsorily purchased from the Potters in 1944.

The farm, under the management of the War Ag, next became a training ground for land girls and a special building was put up on the farm to accommodate them. Columbine Hall became a magnet for the youths of Stowupland. At a funeral wake held in the Columbine Hall barn in December 2016 an old gentleman in a wheelchair told our young gardener, Kate Elliott, that she reminded him of his youth. "We were always coming up here in those days – we were after the land girls," he said.

After the Potters had left, the Ministry of Agriculture appointed Robert Twitchett, formerly of the Prison Service, to manage the farm.

In 1951 William Allan King Rednall was granted the tenancy. He would have liked to buy the farm but, to his disappointment, when it was put up for auction at the Fox Hotel, Stowmarket, in September 1955, it was knocked down for £13,000 to a Norfolk landowner, the Earl of Albemarle, who wanted it as an agricultural investment. Rednall became his tenant but their sons, Allan and Don, finally managed to buy the freehold of the farm in 1977. The Rednalls were to farm the land for 42 years.

In 1992, the Rednall brothers put the Columbine Hall farm up for sale. Their mother had died seven years before. After most of the farmland was sold to neighbouring farmers, the Hall with 29 acres was sold to Hew and Leslie Stevenson in 1993. Columbine Hall's days as a working farm were over and a new life for the old house was to begin.

Owners of Columbine Hall 1730-2018

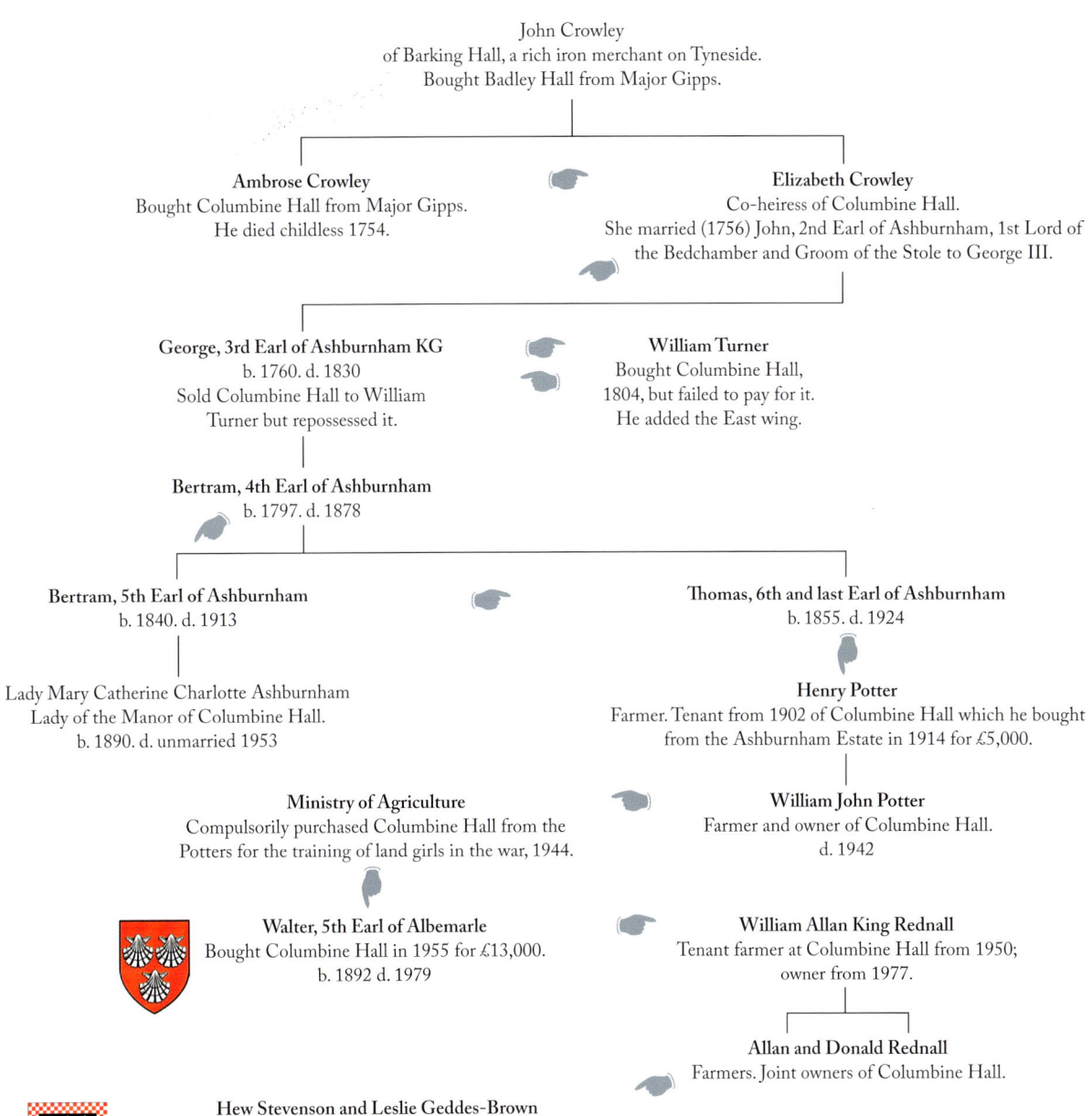

John Crowley
of Barking Hall, a rich iron merchant on Tyneside.
Bought Badley Hall from Major Gipps.

Ambrose Crowley
Bought Columbine Hall from Major Gipps.
He died childless 1754.

Elizabeth Crowley
Co-heiress of Columbine Hall.
She married (1756) John, 2nd Earl of Ashburnham, 1st Lord of the Bedchamber and Groom of the Stole to George III.

George, 3rd Earl of Ashburnham KG
b. 1760. d. 1830
Sold Columbine Hall to William Turner but repossessed it.

William Turner
Bought Columbine Hall, 1804, but failed to pay for it.
He added the East wing.

Bertram, 4th Earl of Ashburnham
b. 1797. d. 1878

Bertram, 5th Earl of Ashburnham
b. 1840. d. 1913

Thomas, 6th and last Earl of Ashburnham
b. 1855. d. 1924

Lady Mary Catherine Charlotte Ashburnham
Lady of the Manor of Columbine Hall.
b. 1890. d. unmarried 1953

Henry Potter
Farmer. Tenant from 1902 of Columbine Hall which he bought from the Ashburnham Estate in 1914 for £5,000.

Ministry of Agriculture
Compulsorily purchased Columbine Hall from the Potters for the training of land girls in the war, 1944.

William John Potter
Farmer and owner of Columbine Hall.
d. 1942

Walter, 5th Earl of Albemarle
Bought Columbine Hall in 1955 for £13,000.
b. 1892 d. 1979

William Allan King Rednall
Tenant farmer at Columbine Hall from 1950; owner from 1977.

Allan and Donald Rednall
Farmers. Joint owners of Columbine Hall.

Hew Stevenson and Leslie Geddes-Brown
(married 1967). Bought Columbine Hall from the Rednalls in 1993.

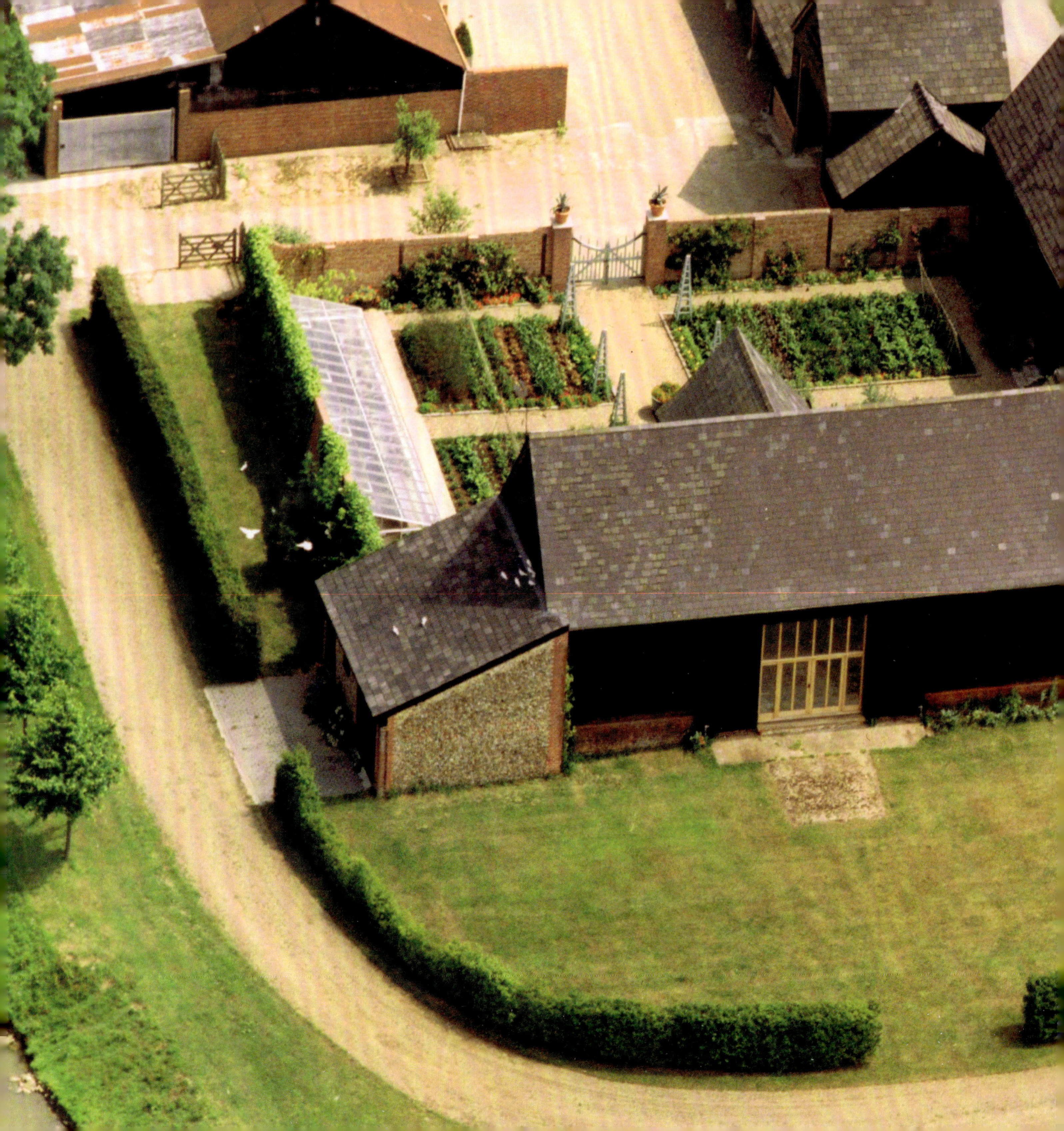

CHAPTER SEVEN

The Gig House and the West Barn

When the house stopped being a working farm there were lots of redundant farm buildings. Most of these were ugly, though practical. Several had asbestos roofs which we needed permission to demolish. The biggest area had its roof removed and its reasonably pleasant brick walls smartened up. Then the concrete floor was dug up (no easy task) and replaced with good quality soil, carefully drained. This became the vegetable garden of four productive beds and climbing roses up the walls. At one side we put in a large greenhouse for tender plants and growing seedlings.

By taking off the barn roof, we displayed two much earlier farm buildings: one a large hay barn made of clapboards with a timbered interior, the second an old stable or store for a gig. These we modernised.

The West Barn is now a place for wedding and other receptions with clever lighting designed by George Carter. It will seat at least 100 people on separate tables. The Half Moon lawn alongside is hard enough standing for a marquee for extra guests. We also built on an annexe, also of clapboard, for caterers. A lean-to hen house adjacent to the barn we made into a smart toilet block. The Gig House we transformed into a holiday cottage for holiday makers, wedding guests and others. Melvyn Smith did the work changing a really messy interior into an open-plan ground floor with three bedrooms for six sleepers above. It has its own small garden and use of all the grounds.

Both have become popular locally with an increasing number of wedding receptions, village parties and teas for when the garden is open.

OPPOSITE ABOVE The six grain silos were sold to a neighbouring farmer.
OPPOSITE BELOW The Gig House was a workshop and store (and a packrat's lair).
BELOW The west side of the West Barn today looks out over the park.
PREVIOUS PAGES The West Barn and Walled Garden. The Gig House holiday cottage is on the right.

ABOVE The Gig House holiday cottage interior as it is today.
RIGHT The West Barn interior. The oil painting, The Courtesan, is after Sigalon.

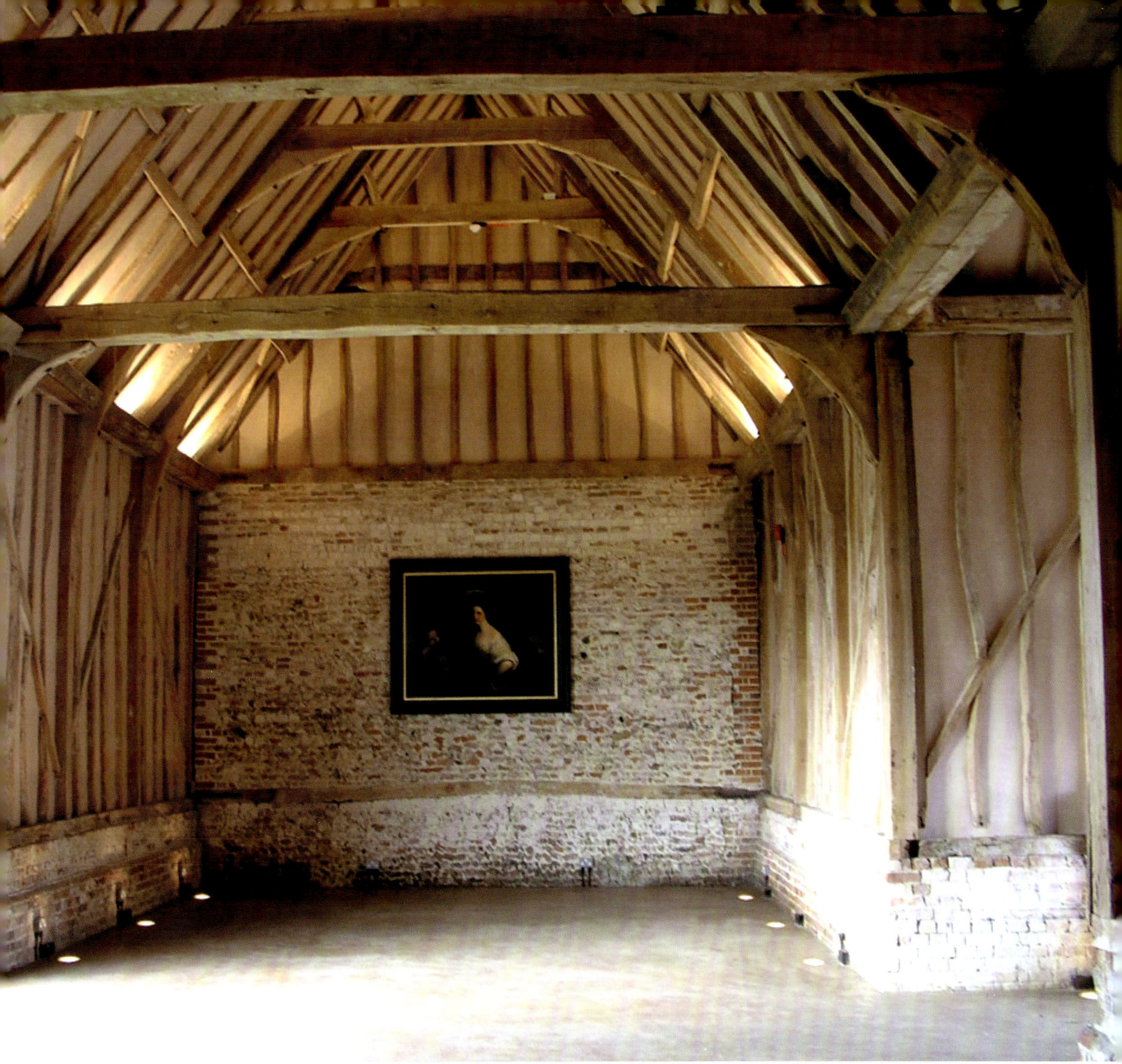

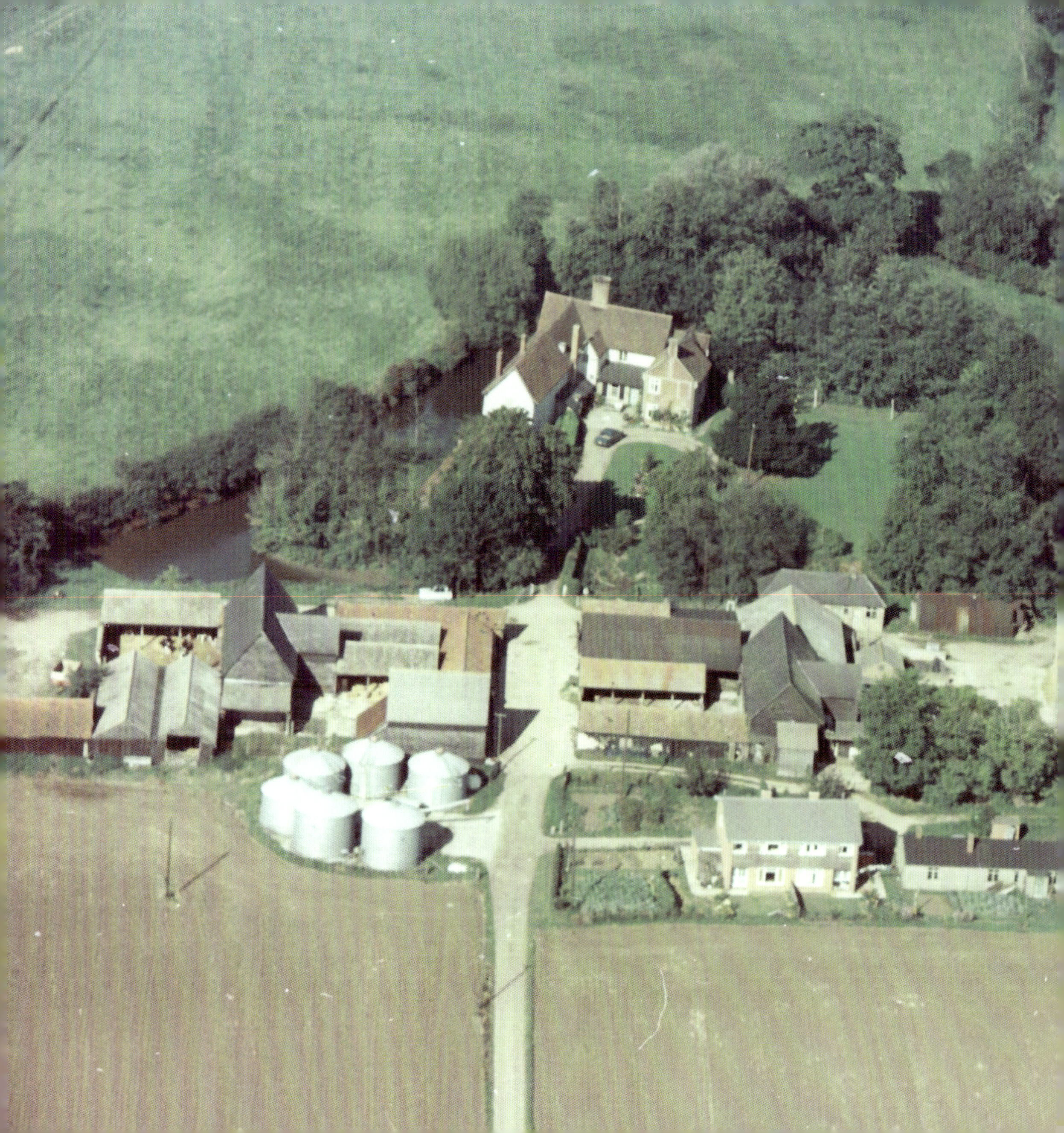

Chapter Eight

How it was

By Hew Stevenson

LEFT Our first years were spent in a sea of mud.
PREVIOUS PAGES Columbine Hall with its farm buildings, c1970

On 24 November 1992, after seeing an advertisement in *Country Life*, we came to view Columbine Hall, a forlorn house with 29 acres near Stowmarket in Suffolk. It was a depressing experience. The old farm house had a truly romantic setting, rising on two of its sides directly out of the waters of a wide and deep moat. But it was a bitterly cold day and the house had been empty since the last farmer's widow had died seven years before. Leslie and I were already exhausted having just been to view another Suffolk house where we were dismayed by the enormously expensive new fitted kitchen that the estate agent had claimed as its main attraction. We hated it.

Columbine Hall was hardly more encouraging. No new fitted kitchen here, but the coldness to the touch of its walls and everything in it told the sad story of a house that nobody lived in. The owner, a Norfolk farmer who, with his brother, had inherited the farm from his widowed mother, showed us gloomily round the icy house and then, with an uncharacteristic flourish of enthusiasm, took us outside to show us the property's "greatest asset", the complex of modern concrete-floored and asbestos-roofed farm buildings – all in "excellent condition". Surely this would tempt us. They were hideous.

Columbine Hall had been on the market for a long time. There had been no takers for the whole farm (about 240 acres) so most of the farmland had

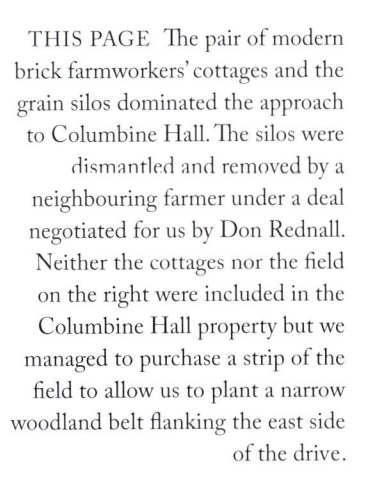

THIS PAGE The pair of modern brick farmworkers' cottages and the grain silos dominated the approach to Columbine Hall. The silos were dismantled and removed by a neighbouring farmer under a deal negotiated for us by Don Rednall. Neither the cottages nor the field on the right were included in the Columbine Hall property but we managed to purchase a strip of the field to allow us to plant a narrow woodland belt flanking the east side of the drive.

RIGHT A view from 1994, when the pleached limes had just been planted.
BELOW English Heritage allowed us to insert an upstairs window in the Regency wing.

ABOVE The yew square has been planted and the faux "bridge" put in place. Overhead electricity cables are now underground.

been sold off separately to neighbouring farmers. The house was now offered with all the farm buildings and its 29 acres. The view from the house to the north was down a pleasing and gently undulating valley but, to the west, there was an unrelenting view of bleak East Anglian prairie, interrupted only by an obtrusive electricity supply line. The characterless drive to the house went in a dead straight line between unfenced ploughed fields. A pair of stark modern brick semi-detached houses, built to accommodate farm workers, and half a dozen enormous grain silos dominated the view as you approached. An old rusting petrol pump, a collapsing Nissen hut and a modern garage made from prefabricated concrete slabs completed the scene. A tangle of electricity and telephone wires stretched from pole to pole across the property.

As we drove dismally back to our London home, Leslie and I indulged in a game of make-believe. Just suppose, we thought, this old house had been in our family for centuries and we had unexpectedly inherited it. It would be sacrilege to sell it. So what would we do (assuming, let's just imagine, that money were no object)?

We would bury the overhead wires; demolish the grain silos, bulldoze away all the concrete and asbestos to reveal the early timber-framed barns, we would plant belts of woodland to conceal the electric supply line on our neighbour's land, we would find a clever way of screening the brick houses, we would lay out a formal garden on the "platform", the acre or so contained within the moat and on which the house stands. We would pull out the modern tiled fireplaces and the linoleum floor coverings inside the house.

But what might all this cost and how long does it take for newly-planted trees to become a wood – in our lifetimes or does it take 50 years? Would £20,000 cover what we wanted to do or are we talking millions? We became very excited. We began to dream. We had to find out some costs to see if our dream had any chance of becoming true. At the end of our two-hour drive to London, and trying hard to conceal our enthusiasm, I telephoned the agents again and arranged to have another look a few days later.

We felt we had to have this house. So, putting on our rose-coloured spectacles, we invited our friend Melvyn Smith, an enthusiastic historic house restorer living in Derbyshire who, we were sure, would fall in love with the house, to come down and crawl all over it and tell us what horrors it might contain. He reported back (as we suspected and hoped he would).

ABOVE George Carter suggested making a feature of this 1960s farm office and dairy on the south side of the moat.
OPPOSITE Melvyn Smith carried out the transformation, re-roofing it, creating new windows, adding the dental cornice and the clock tower in what he described as in the style of Sir Christopher Wren. The building now forms the focal point of an axis through the platform garden and into the countryside beyond.

HOW IT WAS 87

He said it was "wholesome" and that he saw no problems – nothing at all that can't be put right. We also researched the likely cost of planting acres of woods and the cost of bulldozing away concrete. We willed ourselves to find that the project was feasible – so easily persuaded ourselves that it was.

The price asked was £225,000. The agent made no pretence of there being other interested buyers so we cheekily offered £185,000 which was rejected. A few days later we offered £200,000 but the agent told us (as they do) that they were now getting a lot of interest. They decided, to our alarm, to invite sealed bids – best and final offers in writing by a set date. We offered £221,000 and, after a nail-biting week, we were told ours was the winning bid. It was a phone call that changed our lives. I was then 53 and Leslie 51.

ABOVE & OPPOSITE The "bridge" crossing flanked by wooden railings leads to a square gravelled courtyard surrounded by a formal yew hedge.

HOW IT WAS 89

Who We Are

Melvyn
Melvyn Smith's Derbyshire house, Strines Hall, appeared in *World of Interiors* in 1989 and that's how the perfect person to design and build Columbine's interiors was found. He is a designer and craftsman of genius. He panelled the drawing room, uncovered and restored Tudor fireplaces, created built-in bookcases for the library and transformed a derelict outbuilding into a Queen Anne clocktower. He trained as a mechanical engineer but, instead of playing with toy trains marvelled over Gothic cathedrals. He describes his house as 'a series of set pieces' and he pursued the same policy at Columbine. His secret? 'You have to have confidence.'

George
George Carter is a well-known garden designer, who has won several gold medals at Chelsea and recently restored the South Terrace of the Royal Hospital adjacent to the Flower Show site. He has transformed gardens in many countries generally in the 17th century manner, inspired by the gardens of the Baroque era. At Columbine he created a formal garden of yew and hornbeam hedges around a series of courtyards. His aim was to create an impressive entrance to the house and mirror the intricacy of the building's rooms. There are few flowers. 'I've been trying to eliminate colour,' he says of his own garden, 'so the garden is primarily green though I do allow some colours such as grey and white.'

TOP   Melvyn Smith
LEFT   George Carter discussing plans with Hew and Leslie

Kate

Kate Elliott has been in charge of Columbine Hall's garden for over 20 years. She arrived when she was 16 straight from school with no professional qualifications but 'my grandparents were avid gardeners and got me hooked from the age of four.' Since then she was a finalist in 2009's Professional Gardener of the Year, is the National Plant Collection holder for a full collection of narcissus cultivars and is a member of the Chartered Institute of Horticulture and the Professional Gardeners' Guild. Her plant philosophy is is to find 'the right plant for the right place.' 'Columbine is my life,' she adds.

Hew and Leslie

Hew Stevenson's ambition since he was 18 was to create a landscaped garden and park. Columbine Hall's 29 acres including vistas, ancient trees and a wide and deep moat fulfilled this. While George Carter designed the area within the moat, Hew created the vistas into the countryside beyond. Before he retired he was the chairman of Westminster Press, a group of over 100 provincial newspapers. 'Over our 25 years here, it has been wonderful to see our plans on paper fulfilled in the landscape.'

Leslie Geddes-Brown is a writer and journalist, having been arts correspondent of *The Sunday Times* and deputy editor of both *World of Interiors* and *Country Life* (for whom she wrote a weekly column.) She has written 19 books, mostly on gardens and houses along with her other enthusiasm, food and cookery. 'We searched for a house for months and Columbine had it all: it was medieval, unusual and, above all, romantic.'

TOP Kate
RIGHT Hew and Leslie with Otto beside the moat

RIGHT The moat banks are left wild with cow parsley in the spring.

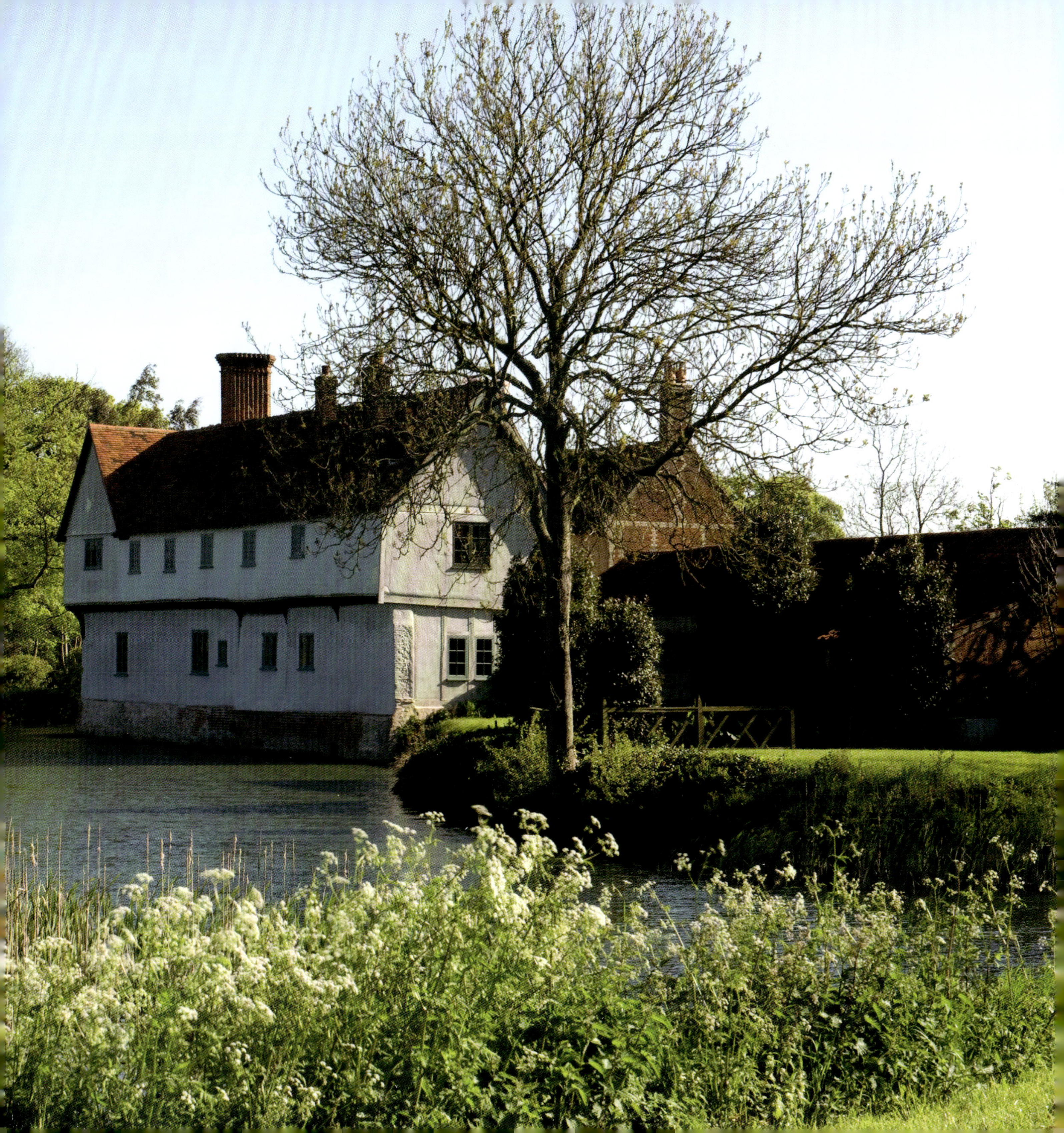

Index

Agriculture, Ministry of 71, 72, 73
Albemarle, Earl of 72, 73
Ashburnham, Earls of 18, 64, 68, 69, 70, 73

Badley hall 63, 64
Barking Hall 64
Boby family 68, 69, 70
Boleyn, Mary 60
Bosmelet, Chateau de 44
Browne, John of Leiston 60

Carey, Sir Robert, Earl of Monmouth 59, 60, 61, 63
Carey, William 58, 60
Carter family of Stowupland 69
Carter, George 24, 28, 31, 32, 38, 76, 86, 90
Collier, William, cartographer 62
Colman, John 59, 63, 64
Columbers family 18, 48, 50
Columbine, variations of name 6
Country Life magazine 37, 82
Crowley, Ambrose 64, 73
Crowley, Elizabeth, Countess of Ashburnham 64, 65, 73

Debla 11

Elizabeth I 60
Elliott, Kate 34, 44, 72, 91
English Heritage 84

Gamberia, La, Tuscany 42
Gardiner, John and Agnes, 58, 59, 60
Geddes-Brown, Leslie 15, 37, 72, 73, 82-88, 91
Gipps, Major Richard 59, 64, 68

Hart, Brian 10 et seq
Hawkins, Juliet 31
Henry VIII 60
Hoare of Bath, William 64, 65

Hotot family 18, 48, 50, 51, 54
Hunsdon, Lord 58, 60

Interiors, World of, magazine 15, 20

Jacob, Samuel 69
James I 63

Keble, Giles 60, 61
King, Ian 12

Land girls 20, 34, 72

McPherson, Ian 10, 11

Operation Pied Piper 10

Peasants' Revolt 50
Pole, Cardinal 42
Poley family 59, 63
Poley, Sir John 18, 63
Potter family 10, 11, 70, 71, 72, 73

Rednall family 20, 72, 73, 83
Rogers, John (Secret Gardens) 41

Shephard, George 12
Smith, Melvyn 20, 23, 50, 77, 86, 90
Stanbridge, Thomas 55, 59
Stevenson, Hew 72, 73, 82-88, 91
Stevenson, Leslie, *see* Geddes-Brown

Turner, William 68, 73
Twitchett, Robert 72
Tyrrell family 18, 48, 54, 55

Whaits, Nicholas 68

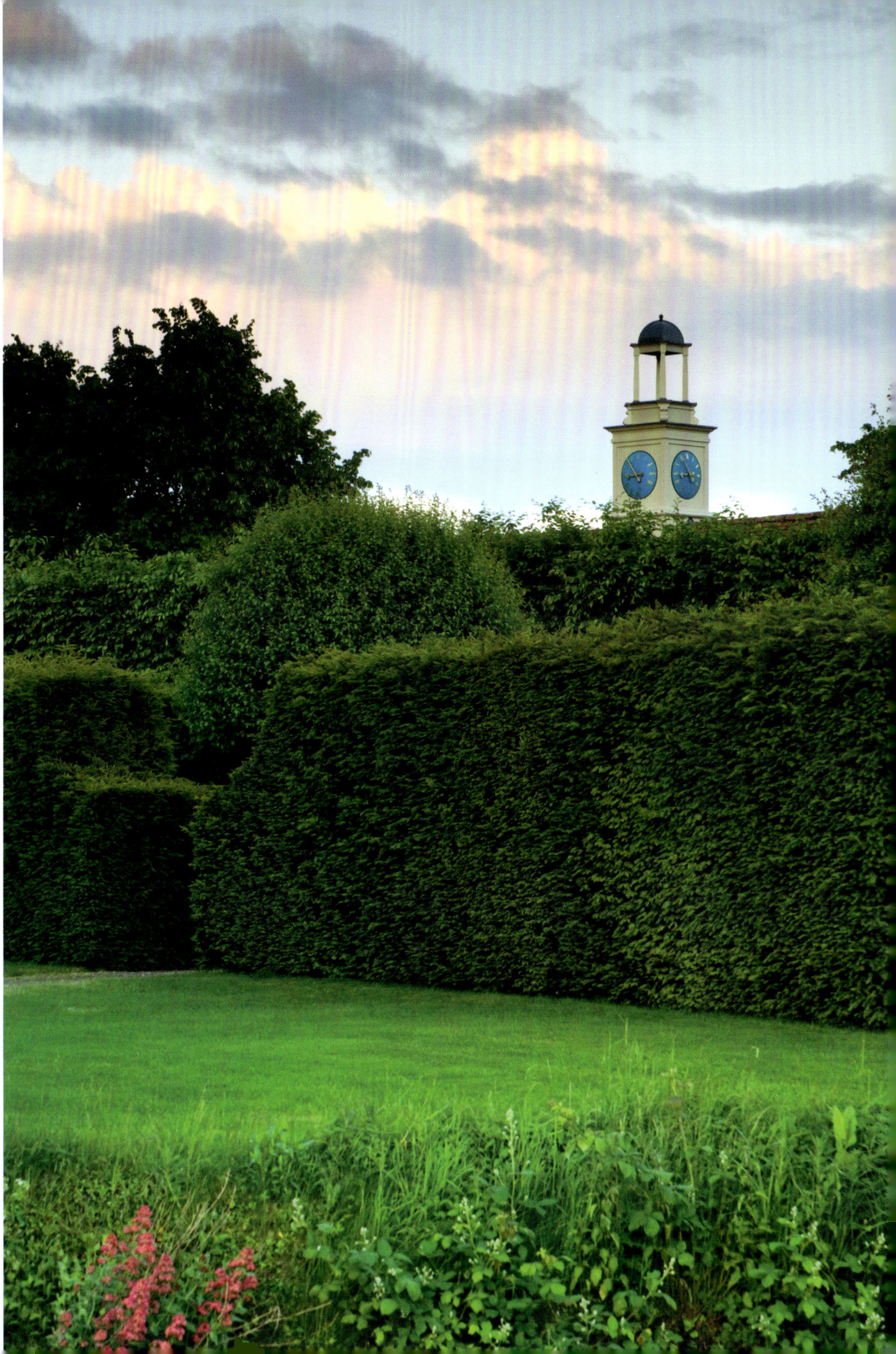

Picture Credits

Kate Elliott front cover, 35, 42, 45
Marcus Harpur 4-5, 14, 19, 32 (top), 33, 36, 37, 40, 43, 89, 92, 95
Brian Hart 11, 12
©*The World of Interiors* magazine (Bill Batten) pre-title page, 18, 20, 21, 22, 24, 25
©Peter Baistow 8, 16, 32 (bottom), 66
©Marianne Majerus 26, 39, 96
George Carter 28
Melvyn Smith 52, 90 (top)
©Eleanor Bentall 91 (bottom)
Philip Aitkens and Nicolaas Joubert 55, 58 (top)
National Trust (Montacute) 61
©Suffolk Photographic Survey 59
The Boby family 70
Valerie Wagnall 72 (top)
Lynn Gallant 72 (bottom)
©*Kitchen Garden Magazine* (Pamela Deschamps) 91 (top)
©*Country Living* (William Shaw) 91 (bottom)

Acknowledgements

We owe special thanks to those who have helped to bring the restoration of Columbine Hall and its lands to fruition, especially Melvyn Smith, George Carter, Juliet Hawkins and Kate Elliott; also to Dennis Barrell, Gareth Knight and Nigel Napier whose contribution to the efforts of maintaining the grounds are invaluable and essential.

We thank Philip Aitken and Edward Martin who have contributed greatly to our knowledge of the history of Columbine Hall.

Thank you to the editors of *Country Life* and *The World of Interiors* for permission to reproduce in this book articles first published in their magazines as well as all those who have contributed photographs to illustrate it. Lastly, we are especially grateful to Maggie Town who has designed the book with skill and imagination.

Town

KING'S

Great Lawn
Y 4

Five
Acre Field
Y. 22

Middle Field
Y. 23

Lower Field